HANDBOOKS FOR RESEARCH IN POLITICAL BEHAVIOR

edited by James A. Robinson, The Ohio State University

ELITE AND SPECIALIZED INTERVIEWING

elite and specialized interviewing

LEWIS ANTHONY DEXTER

NORTHWESTERN UNIVERSITY PRESS • Evanston 1970

To the memory of
MORTON GRODZINS (*d. 1964*)
Chairman, Department of Political Science,
University of Chicago

His capacity for perceptive enthusiasm was unequaled;
a first-rate interviewer, a superb listener, and a creative scholar.
I still frequently find myself saying "I wish I could
tell Morton about that!"

CONTENTS

EDITOR'S FOREWORD

The reader who turns the pages of this book needs no editor's testimony to the contemporary importance of "the interview" as a method of inquiry. Students, scholars, journalists, virtually every writer and reader concerned with social affairs, supplements written records with personal interviews. In the mid-twentieth century, survey research attained high status and wide use among social scientists, notably in measuring and describing large aggregates—national opinions, regional variations, etc. At about the same time, a few scholars of politics and sociology began to adapt the techniques of systematic survey interviewing to smaller populations of elites, including congressmen, lawyers, professors, and physicians. Gradually, experience demonstrated important similarities and differences between elite interviewing and survey interviewing.

Dr. Lewis Anthony Dexter has been among the pioneers whose interviews with elites opened new ideas for scholarly analysis. As one will note from his examples in this book, his "respondents" or "interviewees" are of many kinds, political and nonpolitical, professional and avocational, local and cosmopolitan. From his virtually unique experience, Dr. Dexter has distilled some recommendations for effective use of a respondent's time by a scholarly interviewer.

These recommendations are not enumerated in the manner of a modern travel guide. The sojourner among social elites will find Dexter's style less like a Fielding's or a Fodor's guidebook and more like the reflective essays of an Alec Waugh. The discursive quality that marks this book has almost gone out of fashion in this era of research summaries and technical reports. Except for David Riesman, few social scientists have similarly regarded the interview itself as a social phenomenon of intrinsic interest.

At one time or another in my academic experience, I have interviewed a variety of political elites—candidates, congressmen, bureaucrats, cabinet officials, military officers, diplomats, and presidents. I have been tempted occasionally to distill some principles that run throughout interviews with these different respondents. Yet each time I have seriously begun the task, I have found the principles trivial, commonsensical, simple, one-dimensional, unless put in the context of the social event that the interview constituted. Hence, I have read Dexter's book with admiration for the way in which it illustrates the subtleties of asking questions, recording replies, and drawing inferences in a variety of encounters, some easy, some frustrating.

So, I have found this a manual of wisdom. I have also found it full of humane counsel. The respondent is a human being. Whatever value the scholar may attach to the enlightenment he hopes to acquire through information obtained in the interview, he also ought to place a value on the dignity, privacy, and courtesy of the person who has granted him the interview. Dexter's concern with the moral limits of interviewing deserves the reader's thoughtful attention every bit as much as his examples of craftily successful questioning.

The *Handbooks for Research in Political Behavior* have usually been formal treatises that introduce the reader to a well-traveled terrain. This book, equally useful to students, differs from its bookshelf neighbors. It explores a subject heretofore largely untouched, except for occasional journal articles. Accordingly, Lewis Dexter's book merits the attention of a full company of social scientists, from undergraduate student to advanced specialist.

August, 1969   JAMES A. ROBINSON

ACKNOWLEDGMENTS

Far and away my greatest cumulative indebtedness is to the many hundreds of people who have let me interview them; they have taught me much of whatever I know about many subjects and the greatest part of what I know about interviewing.

In preparing this book, my profoundest direct obligation is to the Harvard University Libraries; having used these libraries, intermittently, for thirty-four years, I have constantly been amazed by the cheerful and competent service which each successive generation of library assistants manages to provide; they are always by far the best argument for working in Cambridge. But on this book in particular, where I had to trace down a great many scattered items, I am sure my good fortune in being able to use these libraries saved me many weeks of work, and helped me avoid a good deal of the exasperation which I would have experienced almost anywhere else.

Those who read the book will note my feeling that I was especially stimulated to think about interviewing as a process by my two Massachusetts Institute of Technology colleagues on the "trade study," Raymond Bauer and Ithiel Pool; I state my acknowledgment to them at greater length on p. 161 of the text. Discussions with David Riesman during the 1950's also helped to develop my concern with the interview process. I have tried to express my gratitude to Morton Grodzins for his encouragement on this as on many other matters in the dedication.

If the book in its present form is worthwhile, it is because of a suggestion by Aaron Wildavsky; I had originally planned a more modest enterprise, but he stipulated that I ought to review the literature.

A number of scholars have been helpful in providing leads, references, documents, and reprints; I am especially obligated to

Donald E. Allen, Albert Biderman, Lindsey Churchill, Raymond Fink, H. R. Glick, Harold Isaacs, Charles Morrissey, Charleton Price, Kenneth Vines, and William Foote Whyte for their help along these lines. My former students, Jeanne Nicholson, now Danforth Fellow in Political Science at Johns Hopkins University, and Irene Moreda, now Fellow in Social Work at the University of Chicago, kindly answered some questions for me. James A. Robinson (now provost of Ohio State University) and his secretarial staff, Anne Trupp, Theresa Loffredo, and Gloria Werth, have been generously helpful. I wish to thank Elizabeth H. Howze for compiling the index.

Comments by Peter K. Manning, Michigan State University, and permission to quote them are much appreciated.

Finally, I am glad to acknowledge permission to use the copyrighted material in Chapter IV from the Oral History Association and in Chapter V from the Society for Applied Anthropology.

Belmont, Massachusetts   L. A. D.
December, 1968

ELITE AND SPECIALIZED INTERVIEWING

CHAPTER I

INTRODUCTION

For Whom Is This Book Intended?
Who Might Find It Useful?

This book was initially designed for *political scientists and sociologists* and also for *professional journalists and other reporters engaged in the collection of information and intelligence for immediate use.* As I worked on it, I came to see that it has especial relevances for *oral historians.* It is pertinent, also, to *literary history and criticism, for the history of science, and military history.* My ideas about elite interviewing and the use of informants have come more from *anthropologists* and *applied anthropologists* than from any other professional group; I hope there will be some feedback in return. Chapter III shows that I started this project as a result of a contemplated study on *legal practice;* there is a prospect of increasing our knowledge of the way laws actually are implemented through improved awareness as to how interviews are conducted and the planned use of informants. There have also been a number of studies in the fields of *educational administration* and *educational sociology* which have relied upon elite interviewing. After writing the book, I came to see how it ought to have value for the practicing physician.[1]

Bingham, Moore, and Gustad[2] in their encyclopedic survey discuss other professions which use interviews of a sort which would be called "elite" or specialized as these terms are defined below. My impression is that, as *social workers* have become more systematically and vividly aware of the social milieu, the situation, the context, they have moved toward awareness of the value of the approaches to interviewing which are here suggested. While ten years ago relatively few social workers would have felt that what is said here would be relevant, a good many will now find something pertinent in the remarks which follow. I am uncertain whether there is anything of use to psychiatrists or clinical psychologists in what is said here; the single most important work in stimulating my own awarenesses about interviewing was Theodore Reik's *Listening with the Third Ear*, and in some respects I have translated what Reik has to say into broader contexts and other perspectives. Whether these contexts and perspectives would be generally helpful for clinical psychologists or psychiatrists, I cannot judge.

However, in the long run—from a *theoretical* standpoint—perhaps the interpretation of the way in which the interviewer learns from the interview will be useful in clinical psychology, psychiatry, and related fields. Indeed, from this theoretic standpoint, the suggestions about how to interpret the interview may be useful (and even on occasion improve validity) in such fact-oriented situations as the interrogation of a neutral observer or expert witness by *a commission of inquiry, a legislative committee, or a detective!* For, in terms of the theoretical approach, almost all use of informants and interviewing of experts and influentials may acquire more meaning by being seen from the standpoint of transactionalists or symbolic interactionists. In a sense, what I am doing is to suggest that the work of Robert Rosenthal and Neil Friedman on the social nature of the research experiment is applicable also to most interviews—whether conducted by a *journalist,* for the sake of hard news; by *an investigator,* for, for instance, *an insurance company,* trying to find out from *experts,* what probably happened in a particular situation; or a research scholar, studying the nature of political behavior somewhere.

Obviously, I would not have written a book such as this one, unless I believed that elite-specialized interviewing is a useful method of data collection. However, I want to stress that there are many times and circumstances when the elite interview is emphatically *not* the technique of choice. I would hope that every one who reads this book also knows Webb, Campbell, Schwartz, and Sechrest, *Unobtrusive Measures;* they report numerous alternatives to the interview on occasions when the current fashion in political science, sociology, and the study of mass communications calls for interviewing—ingenious investigators will no doubt develop further alternatives.

What Is an "Elite Interview"?
What Is an Informant?

Like Riesman (*Abundance*, p. 528 n. 16), "I am not happy with the term 'elite' with its connotations of superiority. Yet I have found no other term that is shorthand for the point I want to make, namely that people in important or exposed positions may require VIP interviewing treatment on the topics which relate to their importance or exposure." Indeed, the only other terms frequently used in the literature are more confusing—"nonstandardized" or "exploratory" or "journalistic."

Riesman's explanation gives a lead as to what is here meant by an elite interview. It is an interview with *any* interviewee—and stress should be placed on the word "any"—who in terms of the current purposes of the interviewer is given special, nonstandardized treatment. By special, nonstandardized treatment I mean

1. stressing the interviewee's definition of the situation,
2. encouraging the interviewee to structure the account of the situation,
3. letting the interviewee introduce to a considerable extent (an extent which will of course vary from project to project and interviewer to interviewer) his notions of what he regards as relevant, instead of relying upon the investigator's notions of relevance.

Put another way, in standardized interviewing—and in much seemingly nonstandardized interviewing, too (for instance, in Merton's "focused interview" in its pure form)—the investigator defines the question and the problem; he is only looking for answers within the bounds set by his presuppositions. In elite interviewing, as here defined, however, the investigator is willing, and often eager to let the interviewee teach him what the problem, the question, the situation, is—to the limits, of course, of the interviewer's ability to perceive relationships to his basic problems, whatever these may be.

Partly out of necessity (see Chaplin), this approach has been adopted much more often with the influential, the prominent, and the well-informed than with the rank-and-file of a population. For one thing, a good many well-informed or influential people are unwilling to accept the assumptions with which the investigator starts; they insist on explaining to him how they see the situation, what the real problems are as they view the matter. Moreover, the interviewer confronted with genuinely prominent people or the prestigious well-informed is unlikely to feel that he can insist on their hewing to a standardized line of discussion. To be sure, James Robinson, as well as Hunt, Crane, and Wahlke, and others, have shown that survey interviewing is, in a sense, possible even with such persons as members of Congress or of a parliament; but actual field interviewers sometimes feel that the most valuable part of what they have been told—that which gives it the fullest meaning—has been discarded. Lerner in his report on interviewing well-informed Frenchmen speaks of their resistance to a "Gallup," i.e., a standardized poll-type interview. He seems to attribute this reluctance directly to something in French culture; since French mass-opinion studies have apparently been successfully conducted for years, I suspect that in France, because of the greater emphasis upon intellectual clarity, exactness, and sharpness, the well-informed and the expert are more precise about formulating the tendency of the well-informed anywhere to resist the oversimplifications of the standardized interview.

Another characteristic of elite interviewing is this: In the standardized interview, the typical survey, a deviation is ordinarily handled statistically; but in an elite interview, an exception, a deviation, an unusual interpretation may suggest a revision, a reinterpretation, an extension, a new approach. In an elite interview it cannot at all be assumed—as it is in the typical survey—that persons or categories of persons are equally important. In interviewing members of a state legislature (as Garceau and Silverman did in Vermont) most of the members may give this or that answer; but it may well be that only a few members give the insightful answers because they are the ones who both know and can articulate how things are actually done. Obviously, some quasi-independent or independent test is desirable in order to believe what they say rather than what the majority says. This test may, however, be simply that of comprehensibility, plausibility, and consistency. An example of where elite interviewing might be significant is suggested by the following, over-simplified example: Suppose most members of a legislature report themselves to be subjected to and influenced by a good deal of "pressure" in regard to a given type of legislation. Suppose other members report relatively little pressure or seem to disregard or discount it. Suppose that the style, manner, experience, and committee and leadership positions of the latter group of members suggest that they had far more weight in determining what legislation was finally enacted than the rank-and-file of the membership. Then, what these latter members report may be more significant in understanding the political system.[3]

Now, in fact, a large number of persons are well-informed or influential on something. The worker whose views on politics or morality can be handled satisfactorily enough by a standardized, survey interview may have taken part in the early days of forming a national trade union, and the oral historian who talks with him about this experience is well advised to give him VIP treatment, that is to give him broad leeway in structuring his recollections of the situation and in recording what he regards as relevant. Or a research scholar such as Lane may choose such a worker, precisely because of his seeming ordinariness, as a subject in an intensive study of the formation of political attitudes and ideas; in such a case, too, he may profitably be encouraged to structure the situation for himself. Indeed, almost any mother of young children is a well-informed expert (with, to be sure, many strong biases) on their current behavior and habits; and for certain purposes, ranging from a journalist's documentary story about child-rearing for a mass magazine to a scholar's study of factors in personality development, an interview with a mother about her children will be, in terms of the definition used here, an elite interview.

An *informant* is, in the common usage of the term, distinguished from an elite interviewee by two factors: participation

and time. The informant is regarded to some, often to a considerable, extent as a subprofessional colleague or co-worker of
the research investigator. Paul speaks of *key informants* as

> ideally . . . individuals who have not only proved themselves
> well informed and well connected, but have demonstrated a
> capacity to adopt the standpoint of the investigator. Informing
> him of rumors and coming events, suggesting secondary in-
> formants, preparing the way, advising on tactics and tact,
> securing additional data on their own, and assisting the an-
> thropologist in numerous other ways.

In other words, the informant, as the term is used by anthropologists, becomes a kind of member of the research team. But,
in general, informants, no matter how close their personal identification with the project, no matter how great their zeal, do
not acquire the full viewpoint of the investigator.

Consequently, the investigator—whether researcher or news-
paperman—will, if he is wise, treat each comment by key informants in the same way as he treats any other item in any
other elite interview. That is, he will assess its meaning, relevance, and value in terms of the informant's social position,
frame of reference, guessed-at purposes, etc. To be sure he often
will know much about the informant's biases and preconceptions,
and, conversely, the informant has had chances to test out and
redefine his conceptions as to what the investigator wants to
learn. However, all this simply means that a skilled investigator
has acquired greater *awareness* of the informant's criteria of
selection and emphasis; other astute and perceptive elite interviewees are likely to be much affected in what they report by
preconceptions about the investigator and by their own biases,
but the investigator has, on the whole, less chance to allow for
these preconceptions and biases.

Concentration on a few key informants may, therefore, help
the investigator to acquire a better picture of the norms, attitudes,
expectations, and evaluations of a particular group than he could
obtain *solely* from less intensive observations or through conducting a greater number of less intensive interviews, by themselves. Naturally, it will often be preferable to combine the use

of informants with other interviewing and with other methods of data collection.

At this point I differ with Scott, who has written one of the few coherent and helpful discussions of how informant reports may be used (pp. 291-94). He says, "treating an informant as a representative member of a subject group is probably the most frequent and at the same time the least defensible use to which such persons are put. . . . Persons willing to assume such a role are likely to be somewhat marginal to their group." Although this point is several times stated in the literature, no evidence is given, and it seems to me to depend upon the values of the group—in a group where contact with scholars or foreigners can confer prestige or pleasure, or where there is a strain of emphasis on self-analysis or teaching, I do not see why the contention would be true. Furthermore, Scott continues, "the more highly differentiated the social system to which the informant belongs— the more likely it is that any given informant will be nonrepresentative of the whole." The United States Congress provides examples of this latter point; since, as Dexter (*Sociology*), and others have pointed out, congressmen are free professionals who can choose their own job definitions and role exphases, there is no guarantee that what Senator X tells you about how he does his job applies to any other senator. Nevertheless, an intensive account, dealing with different situations and different times, from even the most atypical senator with the most atypical staff, of how the job is handled could throw considerable light upon what expectations senators in general meet and fail to meet, what inputs they are ignoring, what potential inputs they are choking off, what frustrations of anticipated relationships they create, and so on. In some instances, study of a rather deviant case—such as Senator Paul H. Douglas (see, for example, Kenneth Gray's account of Douglas's handling of mail)—might even highlight possibilities, expectations, and so forth which would not become so apparent in studying a more representative case.

Obviously, it is desirable to know how representative an informant is. But to a considerable extent, careful analysis of what an informant says, how he views the world, how he views the investigator, etc., will provide clues to the ways he is apt to be unrepresentative, and so as to what is representative. Thus Scott's point can generally be handled.

Scott also says that "even if the informant can be considered representative of his subject group at the beginning of research, the demands of his role as informant—the need for heightened sensitivities towards self and others—will render him unrepresentative before the study is well under way." It seems to me that it is perfectly possible in many instances to use the very process of self-discovery itself as a key or clue to the nature of the social patterns under study; precisely as the informant becomes more self-conscious, less typical, he articulates what he previously took for granted and helps to discover meanings in his group. The kind of excitement engendered by such discovery seems to be a reward in itself to a good many persons; "Doc" and Sam in Whyte's *Street Corner Society* and the several major informants recollected by Powdermaker in her *Stranger and Friend* all seem to have experienced this kind of exciting insight and, in acquiring it, became more (not less) useful informants. (I do not know of any study in which the development of this kind of perception by the informant has been focused upon and systematically traced out—although I think I feel it to some degree in the work of Sutherland and Shaw, perhaps even more clearly in Mintz's beautiful study.)

I would add that an informant may be particularly useful in helping to formulate latent values and latent assumptions. For instance, the term "stupid" and the disagreeable connotations of "stupidity" are characteristic of United States society, but apparently there are a whole bundle of implications in this pejorative notion. I have tried to find out from some of my students in class discussion what it means to them, but I suspect that for careful analysis intensive discussions with a few of them, employing them as informants, would have been more valuable (see Dexter, *Tyranny*). Similarly, were one to try to study "friendship" or "fairness" as central notions in American society, the use of informants would be highly desirable, although the study should of course be supplemented by interviews with a more diverse group and by observation.

Scott says that informants are justifiably used chiefly as (a) surrogate observers, and (b) experts. There are, of course, many observations which, for one reason or another, an investigator cannot himself make; somebody else's report must, for instance, be accepted as to what happens in genuinely secret meetings or sacred, genuinely restricted ceremonies. Similarly, oral historians in particular, and often other social scientists, spend a good deal of time asking people to recollect something that has already happened or something that developed over a long period of time. And, of course, there are many situations which perhaps can be observed by a scholar himself but which demand specialized knowledge or skill to interpret and evaluate. For instance, in various interviews connected with civil defense planning in which I have been engaged (see Dexter, "Civil Defense") I would probably have been more at home and asked more cogent questions if I had had fuller knowledge of shelter technology than I do; an informant or expert adviser of some sort on this matter would have been helpful.

How Do You Know When to Interview, When to Use Informants, etc?

Research demands, as Phillips clearly explains, balancing strategies and tactics in light of overall purposes, both theoretic and practical. In much the same way, the same relationship of purposes and situation determines appropriate tactics for journalists and reporters.

This is to make the obvious point that interviewing is the preferred tactic of data collection when in fact it appears likely that it will get *better* data or *more* data or data *at less cost* than other tactics! The implications of the suggestion, however obvious, are not always followed out; for at a particular time, in particular disciplines, certain research techniques will be in fashion. They will be used, therefore, unreflectively and sometimes inappropriately. At one time the emphasis in political science research was heavily upon legal documentation; now fashions have changed, and many scholars appear to regard interviewing as the "natural" way to tackle any problem involving current data. (Until I read Webb, Campbell, Schwartz, and Sechrest, I was at fault in just this way and consequently wasted time and effort.) Accordingly, what I am here advocating is reflection as to what is the most promising and the least costly technique for obtaining the desired information. In many cases, elite interviewing will turn out to be preferable; I think, for instance, that Bauer, Pool, and Dexter did collect, through interviewing, somewhat more intensive information about politics and "pressure groups" than could have been obtained otherwise. And Sidney and Beatrice Webb give a striking example of a situation where interviewing was advantageous: "By way of contrast we add our account of a leading American politician in the lobby of Congress, which revealed to us something that we had been unable to learn from all the serious studies." They reached conclusions contrary to Woodrow Wilson's in *Congressional Government* (which at the time it was written, 1898, was perhaps the best-known work of political science in the United States). "But he [Wilson] had worked entirely from the printed documents." (Parenthetically, the Webbs here describe themselves as engaging in "personal observation," but actually, as the full extract from their diary shows, they had conducted elite interviews (pp. 185-88). And it is hard to believe that Key, Dollard, and Powdermaker could have contributed to our understanding of southern life as they did by any other means except intensive, specialized interviews.

Had it occurred to me to write such a book as this fifteen years ago, I would have followed up the preceding paragraph by citations of work where interviewing and the use of informants led to significant contributions—the great number of studies reported in *Human Organization* using the approach of William F. Whyte, Everett Hughes, Melville Dalton, and Fritz Roethlisberger are examples. In fact, social anthropologists generally must rely upon informants and interviewees. And I would then have gone ahead to suggest the contributions of interviewing to our knowledge of political behavior and the development of political attitudes through the work of Salter, Lasswell, and others.

For, in 1954, most of us who used interviewing as a major tool for collecting data were still reacting against the old-fashioned social science of the library (the kind which Woodrow Wilson practiced, for instance). The interview put us into the field—

made us feel ourselves to be behavioral scholars. This was particularly true in political science, where—with the exception of the study of votes, obviously limited to a few situations, and the effort at content analysis—no other empirical tool of any great promise was being used. Of course, interviewing as such goes back a long way—back to Lord Bryce or, for that matter, back to the Greeks—but emphasis upon empirical methods of investigation (which in practice generally meant interviewing) as symbolizing a new political science, was a characteristic of the early 1950's.

Now, as Margaret Mead points out—and as Hegel in a more general sense did before her—"no sooner is a preliminary skirmish won [in an intellectual field]—critics and opponents convinced of the validity of some position—than before the grass has grown green again on the battlefield, one has to be off a-pace to start a skirmish against those who have accepted the new idea too thoroughly and too well. . . . The new battle often has to be fought long before most people have become familiar with the last victory." (In Dexter, "Use," I developed this point of Mead's with reference to social science research.) Thus, those of us who spent our youth arguing for an empirical behavioral political and social science have helped to create an overemphasis upon the interview which, in its turn, must now be qualified. As Stein shows (referring particularly to the survey interview, but the same comment applies to elite interviewing, library research, or any other one research tool), "the logic of any method lends itself to a thought-stopping role if it is consciously or unconsciously presumed to be the necessary or exclusive method" (p. 214).

The answer to the question which heads this section may in part be put in terms of the points made by Stein and by Phillips. Interviews should be undertaken, informants should be relied upon, when it is clear that the following conditions can be approached: (a) alternative techniques have been seriously considered in terms of the research issues, (b) the research issues have tended to determine the selection of techniques, rather than the reverse, and (c) inferences drawn from the interviews can be subjected to some sort of independent criticism, or, preferably, vigorous test.

The last point demands a little comment. In much public opinion interviewing, such testing is usually ignored (except in regard to political campaigns and some market research) because, practically speaking, it is difficult to devise and because, if one is narrowly concerned with "opinion," it is not necessarily important. Of course, when election predictions or market-research studies involving consumer behavior are involved, there is a test, and the test is very important. But in any case, in both survey and elite interviewing, the natural tendency of the researcher is to concentrate on the interviews.

Now, where the interviewer, the chief investigator, knows a good deal about the topic—as is hopefully but not universally the case—he can make appropriate discounts for interviewee statements by reference to other sorts of data—including "common sense," common knowledge, and so forth. In many instances, different interviewees, especially if selected with such a possibility in view, can be used to check and correct one another. But, nevertheless, studies are increasingly made where the interviewer-investigator has little independent knowledge; for example, the writing of these pages was interrupted for a conversation with a doctoral candidate (who has already published some of his conclusions) who insisted that certain self-serving statements made by the head of a particular organization were credible because he "knew" the latter would tell the truth. The only supporting evidence lay in the formal rules and manuals of the organization; the thesis-writer had not made any observation or collection of other relevant data, and he himself had had no important direct contact with the organization. It should be noted that the statements of the officials do not, in fact, conform to generally accepted impressions about how such organizations operate.

A far more significant and dramatic example of the difficulty in relying upon interviews as sources of credible data is found in some of the reputational studies of influence. (See Hunter, and also Polsby's criticism of Hunter *et al.*) The scholars engaged in such studies certainly did learn who were reputed to be influential; but much of the argument revolves around the validity of such reports about reputations.

This point is a difficult one to discuss by reference to the literature because a great many, probably the majority, of scholars who ostensibly rely upon interviews or upon an informant as their chief source of data actually have a good deal of independent knowledge about the situation. For instance, Mintz's *Worker in the Cane* is ostensibly a life-history of one informant, but it in fact shows that Mintz had learned much about rural Puerto Rican life, which helps make this life-history meaningful and significant. Also, in Bauer, Pool, and Dexter and in other writings about Congress, I sometimes appear to rely chiefly upon interviews, but in fact I was living in Washington at the time, spent much of my "free" time in a congressional office, saw a good deal of several congressional assistants and secretaries socially, worked on other matters with several persons actively engaged in relationships with Congress (lobbying and liaison), had participated in a number of congressional campaigns, had read extensively about congressional history and behavior, and had some relevant acquaintance with *local* politics in several congressional districts.[4] All these factors made my analysis of interviews somewhat credible. And, as I look back, interviews sometimes acquired meaning from the observations which I often made while waiting in congressional offices—observations of other visitors, secretarial staffs, and so forth. And, finally, most important of all, it happened that interviews with constituents, lobbyists, congressmen of different views and factions, could be and were checked and rechecked against each other. Yet in the book we say little about all this, and in fact it is only now, in 1968, that I realize how much these other factors affected what I "heard."

In sharp contrast is the interviewing in which I have recently been engaged—interviewing with officials in several states and Canadian provinces about administrative frictions and controversies in such fields as health, mental health, and child guidance. Some of the individual interviews are interesting; but I have learned very little by watching or observation. Perhaps this is because I have not stayed long enough in any one state or province, perhaps because this sort of observation does not prove as revealing in bureaucratic offices as in Congress, or perhaps, of course, because for some reason I am not as attuned or as perceptive as I used to be! Although I have a general acquaint- ance with relevant problems, and have had some parallel experi- ences in Massachusetts, I lack most of the advantages which I had in studying Congress. So far, I have learned little out of which I can make coherent sense. For my interviewing to be worthwhile, I have got to see it fit into a pattern, a framework— or I have got to resort to other techniques of collecting data or make clearer to myself what my problems are.

One other example of the tendency to rely heavily upon the interview: over the past couple of years I have attended several meetings with a dozen political scientists engaged in planning a comparative study of state legislatures. Every single discussion, so far as I can recollect, has simply taken for granted the fact that we will rely chiefly upon interviewing (*I as much as the others have done so*). Yet, questions should have been raised about using other methods to learn about legislatures.

Now, in fact, interviews may well lead to valuable analyses of legislatures; but, if so, it will be because of one or the other (or both) of the following factors: either the interviewer will have had a good deal of relevant previous experience which enables him to interpret what he hears and ask meaningful sup- plementary questions, *or* the interviewer will be able to observe and/or take part in the group life of some legislators or lobbyists so that he comes to know what is meaningful to ask and to record. Whyte's report on his experiences in the *Street Corner Society* study are relevant: "Doc" (his principal informant) said to him: "If people accept you, you can just hang around and you'll learn the answers without even having to ask the questions."

Whyte comments:

> I found that this was true. As I sat and listened, I learned the answers to questions that I would not even have had the sense to ask *if I had been getting information solely on an interview- ing basis.* [Italics supplied.] I did not abandon questioning al- together of course. I simply learned to judge how and when to question (pp. 29-30).

This leads up to a final point to be made about when to use interviewing and when to seek for informants. Exploratory or trial interviews of course may be tried out as an experiment to find out how much one knows or can quickly pick up about the background and the situation; in some interviews I conducted with doctors about medical advertising and the effectiveness of detail men, it was, for instance, a surprise to me to discover how much I knew that I had not realized I knew which enabled me to make sense out of these interviews. On the basis of such experiences, I was probably justified in trying out the interviewing with state and provincial officials described above; but when it became apparent that I really did not have enough background to make sense out of them, I should have quit (or postponed the effort until somehow I had acquired the ability to make more of a pattern out of them).

But no one should plan *or finance* an entire study in advance with the expectation of relying chiefly upon interviews for data *unless the interviewers have enough relevant background to be sure that they can make sense out of interview conversations or unless there is a reasonable hope of being able to hang around or in some way observe so as to learn what it is meaningful and significant to ask.* In fact, one should probably go one step further—such expectations may prove to be incorrect (this is just what happened to me in the state-provincial study; I did not "know" as much as I thought I did). *Therefore, any planning for a study assuming a heavy reliance upon elite interviews should have a contingency plan—an escape hatch, an alternative— so that if the elite interviews prove basically uninformative some other techniques can be substituted.* One reason why I gradually withdrew from the projected study of state legislatures, mentioned above, is that I do not see how (practically) such a shift would be feasible; in a study involving ten different states on a somewhat comparable basis it might be difficult to alter techniques.

There are other reasons than inability to make sense out of what the informants say that may make interviewing prove unrewarding as a research technique. In 1966 I undertook about two dozen interviews with civil-defense planning and municipal officials in a particular metropolitan area about their preparation for disaster. The interviews are, I think, good, meaningful, and significant from several standpoints. But they are, in a way, too good. The only way in which I can yet see how to use them would be to publish them with comments and interpretations as they are; and to do so would of course be to violate our promise of confidentiality and unforgivably to embarrass the interviewees. So, I may have to wait until many men younger than I die or retire!

When interviewing does not work, one alternative will be to seek informants—people like "Doc" in *Street Corner Society* or the various informants warmly praised by many anthropologists, such as Powdermaker. But in a complex modern society such as ours it is not always possible to find perceptive informants. Somewhere there may be such people; as I think back over my efforts on the state-provincial study, what I was doing in part was to try to locate informants. I did not get any leads in most of the states or provinces; in the few cases where I learned of people temperamentally equipped to be informants, their political or administrative obligations were such that I could see no way of inducing them to act as informants in depth and detail.

I have devoted a good deal of this discussion to occasions when interviewing should not be relied upon as the technique of choice. As indicated, I have done this on the assumption that people who read any such book as this are predisposed to favor interviewing; if I were sure that all my readers would, for example, be economists or literary critics, I would devote more effort to accentuating the positive. For in those fields—with such occasional exceptions as Hall and Hitch or Katona among economists, or Aaron among literary critic-historians—there has been far too little use of the interview.

In general theoretic terms, Braybrooke, in sharpening and clarifying a familiar distinction, perhaps suggests when elite interviewing is desirable as part of the research inquiry. He distinguishes between *action* and *behavior*. An event is interpreted in action terms when its meaning, to some of the actors involved (in terms of rules, codes, norms, affects, aspirations), is a central focus. (Behavioral reports, on the other hand, may disregard the meaning to the actors.) When meaning is in some sense problematic—when we really cannot be sure what interpretation of what code, norm, affect, rule, etc., guiding the actors, and when this matters—when we do not know their definition of situations— then interviews are often desirable.

But the interviewer must have some capacity to catch the interviewee's meanings, to perceive the framework within which he is talking, if he is to get much out of the interview. Otherwise, he is merely recording verbal behavior; he lacks the capacity to "listen with the third ear." This leads to a concluding point, applicable especially to teachers (and their students) when a classroom requirement schedules a set of elite or depth interviews. More often than not, probably, these are wasteful and an imposition on the interviewee. Because, more often than not, the interviewer-student does not have enough background, enough knowledge, and enough sensitized imagination to catch the subtleties and complexities of what the interviewee is saying. In the first "research" interview I ever conducted—as an undergraduate at the University of Chicago, in an effort to find out something about how some ministers tackled certain problems of peace action—I was largely unfitted to understand what I was told. Having been brought up as a Unitarian, studying in the secularized social-science atmosphere of the University of Chicago, I simply brushed aside statements about religious belief as irrelevant rationalizations; in making my attitude clear to interviewees (and in failing to record what they said) I simply did not let myself learn. Similarly, in the past several years— because I have, for instance, been active in Massachusetts state politics—I have been interviewed by several students, graduate and undergraduate. In most cases, it seems to me they have tried to make the story I reported to them more coherent, more "rational," than in fact it was (as experienced by my associates and me in campaigns and in the Governor's office). Some of the interviewers' imputations seem to have been that we acted in terms *of* power-oriented politics; other imputations were, I think, more oriented toward some kind of norm derived from administrative theory. But, in either case, the interviewers wanted answers reporting sharply motivated behavior, whereas in fact, so far as I could recollect, we acted in response to a complex and often inchoate set of desires and beliefs which could not be stated sharply. My picture of how we acted may have been quite wrong and the interviewer's overall interpretation quite right. But in order to encourage me as an interviewee and to get my interpretation straight, it would have been desirable to use my frame of reference. The only person who has interviewed me about Massachusetts politics and has done this well is Murray Levin. His final interpretation is far sharper than what I would have made had I written the story; but, while interviewing me, he heard me. Other interviewers did not.

At any event, a course which requires or recommends elite interviewing by students should stress the importance of getting a good deal of background *and* of getting the student to try to listen to the interviewee's frame of reference. The phrase is deliberate; a large part of listening with a third ear is noting and adapting to a frame or reference different from one's own. One of the most general difficulties for students, I suspect, will be that suggested in the last paragraph; the experienced person in any field knows that things happen in a subtle, confused, foggy, complex way, which cannot be stated or codified simply; the person without practical experience and without much contact wants to sharpen and simplify.

NOTES

[1] The role of interviewing in medicine became more evident to me because of a period of emergency hospitalization, which interrupted the final draft of the book. I was appalled by the number of medical histories I was asked to give and the carelessness with which they were collected by physicians of some reputation as well as by recent medical school graduates. Questions were repeatedly asked as to which I could have no possible knowledge and where—in order to satisfy the expectations of the interrogators—I had to make the wildest sort of guess (e.g., about diseases of relatives of whom I have seen little of or who have been dead for many years). Many of the questions asked me about my own physical experiences called for close observation of a type which I have never made—a close observation and an accurate recollection. Furthermore, the sheer bulk of the questions, and the number of issues raised, almost certainly led some of these interrogators to overlook what may well have been the most relevant factors in creating the condition from which I was suffering (factors whose significance did not occur to me until after I left the hospital). It was also apparent that most of

the interrogators were not listening to answers anyway. Thinking back over medical check-ups and other visits to doctors in times past, I realize that what I became aware of in the hospital is characteristic of much medical practice (unless some of the supposedly better specialists and general practitioners in the Boston area are untypical of physicians elsewhere). It may indeed be that there is little to be learned from medical histories (although in some cases they may serve as a kind of placebo!), but if this is so it is an enormous waste.

On November 6, 1968, the *New York Times* carried a story, quoting Allan Enelow, Chairman, Department of Psychiatry, Michigan State University, to the effect that (a) interviewing is one of the most important skills for the physician, because of its bearing on getting a medical history, and (b) most medical students learn little about it as a skill.

[2] As a general rule, citations are given in the text simply by the last name of the author(s)—if it is necessary to distinguish one work from other publications of the same author, an identifying word is given. A list of all publications referred to, plus some others, is given at the back of the book with some annotations.

[3] In essence, reflection over a period of fifteen years on the interviews reported in Bauer, Pool, and Dexter, and Dexter, "Representative," and Dexter, *Sociology*, has led me essentially to the point stated in the text. Theoretically, the point can be explained in terms of input and attention factors; the more significant members of any legislative body are apt to receive a greater variety and number of inputs; therefore the frame of reference within which they attend to any given input is less focused and concentrated and of necessity is more comparative in nature; so they are less apt to experience "pressure" where their less significant colleagues would. (I hope to develop the issues here in a discussion of "Politics: Who Attends to What, When, and How," based on the latter part of my forthcoming Rand McNally book, *The Sociology and Politics of Congress*.)

[4] And, of course, my colleague, Ithiel Pool, had also had a great deal of relevant experience and contact.

Frank Bonilla, who was assigned to edit the original draft of my portion of *American Business and Public Policy*, commented at one time that it was difficult to do because so much of it was "autobiographical." At the time I did not know how to take this remark; but looking back, thinking about the sets of experiences which contributed to it, I think this was true—and is or ought to be true of much serious work in our field.

Paul Lazarsfeld and Herbert Hyman objected rather strenuously to my portion of this book because it had no methodological statement. I assumed—and still assume—that they desired the kind of methodological statement often found in their work and that of their students, which has been well criticized by Stein. But in a broader sense, they were quite correct: a spelling-out of the factors leading me to rely upon the interviews, along the lines of what I have just said in the text, would have been helpful to scholars (though it might have made the book altogether too unwieldy).

CHAPTER II

SUGGESTIONS FOR GETTING, CONDUCTING, AND RECORDING THE INTERVIEW

This chapter is described by its title. Chapter III consists of a set of suggestions *about a specific project*—Chapter IV of a report *on another project*. Naturally, there is some overlapping; it seemed useful to repeat and emphasize some points within these different contexts. Chapter V and VI deal with the theory of the interview; again, there is some overlapping, because the earlier chapters depend, logically, on the theory. In view of the fact that more readers are likely to be interested in immediate applications, it seems wiser to start out with the practical chapters; this ordering may also be justified by the fact that experience shows that writers frequently make sensible practical suggestions but go astray theoretically.

The most nearly universal rule for elite and specialized interviewing is that *the best way to interview in a concrete situation depends upon the situation (including the skills and personalities of the interviewers).* Phillips, in a text on *Social Research,* subtitled *Strategy and Tactics,* emphasizes that the investigator must be liberated "from undue reverence for any particular method . . . [he must] make maximal use of his knowledge of the particular research situation facing him" in order to develop situationally relevant strategies. Ultimately, of course, such an approach leads to the point already alluded to, and illuminated by Webb, Campbell, Schwartz, and Sechrest—that there should be careful consideration of *alternatives* to interviewing in each specific situation; otherwise, one gets the tendency exemplified in two recent psychology graduates who came around to see me about possible employment when I was setting up a small wartime intelligence unit in 1942. They were very patriotic and eager to do anything they could to win the war—that is to say, anything at all which permitted them to use Rorschach tests! Other ways of gleaning intelligence left them rather contemptuous of governmental anti-intellectualism!

But, having once *tentatively* decided that interviewing is the best approach (and such a decision should remain tentative as long as practically possible), there are still a number of alternative ways of interviewing. Indeed, there are no universal rules about how best to conduct an interview, excepting only "It depends. . . ." What may be suicidal or impractical for one interviewer or in one situation may be feasible or even the best way to proceed for another interviewer or in another situation. A manual about interviewing is logically like a manual on how to play tennis or how to conduct warfare; no writer of a tennis manual can tell his readers how to win, and no Jomini or Clausewitz can show young officers a certain route to victory. But such writers can suggest some of the issues and tactics which are worth thinking about, and consideration of which can make victory somewhat more likely.

To illustrate the point, I will skip ahead of the logical order of the chapter, and discuss a few issues:

What Sort of Relationship Should the Interviewer Establish with the Interviewee? All "Answers" Depend upon Variables in Concrete Situations. The Use of Leading Questions

This discussion is placed here because it happens to illustrate particularly clearly the point that *who* is interviewing *whom* and *for what purpose* determines what it is best to do. That is to say, "It depends."

Every suggestion about how to conduct interviews must depend upon these all-important variables: the personality and skill of the interviewer, the attitudes and orientation of the interviewee, and the definition by both (and often by significant others) of the situation. For example, it is widely assumed that interviewees are doing interviewers a favor and that, accordingly, interviewers must be reasonably courteous and deferential to interviewees. Yet, in a stimulating discussion of interview techniques, Nadel (relying primarily upon his field work in Africa), says (p. 323):

> In the case of interviews which bear on secret and forbidden topics, I have found it profitable to stimulate the emotionality of a few chief informants to the extent of arousing almost violent disputes and controversies. The expression of doubt and disbelief on the part of the interviewer . . . induced the key informant to disregard his usual reluctance to speak openly.
>
> A "bullying" technique of this type amounts to the deliberate introduction of leading questions, a practice against which field workers are frequently warned. . . . The risks which this technique involves are not negligible. . . . It should only be used when the interviewer has a good working knowledge of the group and its culture. The culture of the tribe in which I successfully employed it is characterized by marked individual competition, jealousy, and vanity. The same technique might fail completely in a group where these incentives are less strongly pronounced. (It might also fail if applied by interviewers whose own psychological characteristics did not easily lend themselves to turning interviews into tense, duel-like affairs.)

Aside from the temperamental characteristics of the interviewer or interviewees, it might also fail because of the interviewer's social stimulus-value. Daniels, in an extraordinarily insightful report on her experience, shows that an effort to bully her military officer informants would not have worked! Indeed, Nadel was reporting on pre-1939 experiences; but would a white man dealing with a younger generation of anticolonial, freedom-venerating Africans be able to use the same technique safely?

Dexter ("Role") put forward a viewpoint very different from that of Nadel. I argued in that article that the interviewer should try to get cooperation by deliberately seeking to establish "neutrality on the interviewer's side" using the interviewee's value-loaded phraseologies and appearing to adopt, as far as he is able, the interviewee's orientation. I argued for

> sympathetic understanding, so that the interviewer can without strain, talk the informant's language. . . . Even if it is not well done, the effort may promote good feeling. The academically trained interviewer who reassures supporters of Senator

Joseph McCarthy [and] tries to intimate his sympathy with the viewpoint that Eisenhower is being befooled and misled by "the same old State Department gang" will sound clumsy; but he is more likely to be regarded as "having the right spirit" than criticized for awkwardness or insincerity.

Now, for the *kind* of circumstances with which I was concerned at that time, the technique was probably desirable; and it was worth recommending to social scientists in order to help them overcome the suspicion with which they are regarded by members of many groups whom they regard as reactionary or seriously mistaken. In the article, I said that this approach would help social scientists overcome their negative stimulus-value. To me, and perhaps to other interviewers the technique was also valuable because it led us to *listen* to what some interviewees were basically trying to say rather than misinterpreting them in terms of our own assumptions.

But there are numerous occasions when the technique I recommended there will not work. Some social scientists, identified as such and connected with a well-known establishment university, might find the technique boomerang if they tried it out on really committed members of the Ku Klux Klan, for example; they would simply convict themselves of hypocrisy or espionage. I am sure, too, that there are a good many social scientists who could not bring themselves to express sympathy with fundamentalists or antifluoridationists or French-Canadian nationalists but who could obtain data from some of these types by other conversational styles, under specified circumstances. Peter K. Manning (in a letter to me on December 3, 1968) suggests that my 1956 article was overstated in its published form because

one might use leading questions with a tactic of either neutrality or non-neutrality, and . . . these leading questions . . . might be a source of some imputed negative identity to the interviewer as anti-informant. . . . While you have made the logical case that neutrality on the side of the interviewee is sometimes useful, one might make the logically possible, but contrary, argument that some anti-informant questions might be useful to get "polar points" in some issue-related interviewing. This might be called "anti-informant neutrality," which is what often happens anyway [but] *it* might lead to the informant "telling what is needed."

. . . I question whether one could (in general) mount a strategy with any success which was based upon being "anti-informant," [but it] might work . . . where a minority interviewer (e.g., a Negro) was engaged in confrontational tactics, and wanted to find out how far he could go vis-à-vis white liberals. Or, more abstractly, any situation where one wanted to use some sort of guilt or obligation [or, I would add, prestige or fear] which the interviewee owed the interviewer, e.g., psychotherapy, black militant-white liberal, bill collector. . . .

We agree . . . that neutrality on the side of the interviewee or against him might each be useful in some settings, *but the interviewer must be well aware of his self-selected identity* [italics supplied].

The point then is that these central issues of the interview—manifest attitude towards the interviewee, whether to use leading questions, and, if so, what kind of leading questions—will depend upon many variables. The only universal requirement is that the interviewer, in analyzing the interview, should try to determine what tactics he did in fact employ and make at least an informed guess as to how the chosen tactics may have affected what the interviewee said. (Of course, in a world ideally arranged for social scientists, we would systematically try out different tactics with the same interviewee. One reason why, later on, I emphasize the importance of comparing interview reports by different interviewers [on, e.g., the same congressman] is that this may help us begin to see how different tactics make a difference. See p. 160, below.)

The interviewer should be aware, intuitively at least, of different possibilities in terms of the situation, and he must include in the situation his own personality.[1] I would not, fifteen years ago, have dared to use the Nadel technique because I would have feared letting the "duel-like manner," the desire to win in an argument, get the better of me. I have, in fact, never used it; but, as I have grown older, I am less driven to press for verbal victory in an argument; and, as I have had more experience in politics, I find myself less inclined to the irony which, when employed by scholars, is far more distasteful to many interviewees than combativeness. In other words, because I am a different person now than when I wrote the article, I could now employ somewhat different tactics, possibly even, on some occasions, the Nadel technique.

Can Interviewers Get to See Hoped-For Interviewees?
How Do You Introduce Yourself?
How Do You Get People to Grant You Interviews?

The question, naturally, concerns a great many beginning interviewers. On the whole, it appears to be—at least in the United States and Canada—surprisingly easy to obtain interviews with members of elite and specialized groups. Heard, for instance, reports that out of 506 southern politicians of prominence or knowledge whom he and his associates tried to see, only 3 refused to give an interview! (p. 891) I myself was not, as I recollect, turned down by any single business or community figure in Cumberland, Frederick, or Hagerstown, Maryland, whom I tried to see in connection with the trade study; and the five persons who turned me down in the state of Delaware were the most marginal, the least important prospective interviewees (and I could probably have got three of them to see me, had I thought it worthwhile to pursue the kinds of approaches discussed below). Also, in November, 1967, when I was conducting a series of interviews to update my background for my book, *How Organizations Are Represented in Washington,* I do not think I was really turned down by any of the association officials whom I tried to see; and of the sixty-odd people I approached in connection with the Grodzins study of state-federal relations in Maryland and Massachusetts, only one turned me down (and he was an old-time political "associate" of mine who probably would have seen any other interviewer on the same project!). Even in trying to interview physicians for a commercially financed study about the effectiveness of detail men and medical advertising, with a typically short notice I saw about 70 per cent of those whose names were given me as first choice, and in the other cases saw a second or third choice without fail.

Most interviewers in the United States, as far as I know, would find that Isaacs (pp. 29-30) expresses their experience as follows:

I was met by fewer than half a dozen refusals whereas scores of stereotypically rushed and busy Americans, often in high places, stopped to give a stranger two hours or more of their time to answer questions that entered into quite deep areas of their life histories, experiences, and states of mind. I had the repeated experiences of entering such a man's office—or, in many cases, his home—with no other introduction than my previous letter, and of plunging him, in a matter of minutes, into a process of self-examination, which was often new, arousing, and disturbing to him. There was . . . an implicit understanding of the usefulness and importance of participating in research, an automatic acceptance of the good faith of the pledge of confidence, a notable degree of candor, a free and interesting yielding to the spirit of inquiry. This was most impressive in itself, quite apart from the merits of these individuals or the quality or content of the ideas they turned out to hold. In more ways than one, these 181 men and women have been my teachers.

It would, of course, be unwise to rely entirely upon published reports of "successful" studies. Powdermaker tells us (p. 216) that she was unable to meet *anyone* in the front offices in Hollywood, the people who, in a sense, were reputed to run the industry which she was studying! Kincaid and Bright discuss with feeling their problems in getting to see business leaders in connection with a civil defense study. Roy recounts an attempt where the majority of his efforts to get meaningful interviews were failures apparently because union organizers believed him to be either a management spy or someone sent in by national headquarters to check on their efficiency, whereas management supporters believed him to be pro-union or someone sent in from above to check on the way local management was handling the union! (This experience occurred after he had engaged in a number of research projects in which he had been successful in getting interviews.)

It is altogether natural that there should be no statistics as to how many interviewers experience refusals and how many proportionally succeed in seeing most or all the people whom they planned to see. But, so far, the proportion who succeed in getting needed interviews is almost certainly much greater than the proportion who fail.

It is, of course, true that there are a number of persons who, in actual fact, are overcommitted or who, for some professional reason, are unable to schedule appointments readily when you wish to see them. For example, although I do not think I was really refused by any of the association representatives whom I tried to see in November, 1967, about one-fourth of all the persons I approached were actually out of town during the month, or were engaged in rush activities in connection with legislation just then being finalized by the Congress, or were in some other—I judge, quite genuine—way overburdened during the four weeks I spent on the project. Similarly, top state government officials may be all tied up during a budget period; and so on. It is usually possible to find out when the pressure will be off, if your own time permits it.

There are, also, of course, individuals who, for personality reasons, find it difficult to keep to a schedule or who chronically overcommit themselves; it is ordinarily possible to get to see them, though in such cases it may be necessary to circumvent a protective secretary or assistant. (I wonder whether part of Powdermaker's difficulty in getting to see the top brass in the movie industry may have been lack of experience in circumventing secretaries—something with which her previous field work in a stone-age culture and in a small town in Mississippi would have not supplied her!)

The kind of situation which Roy describes could, of course, altogether stymie one's chances of getting needed interviews (although I have heard of few parallels); even here, however, he was partly able to recoup by getting introductions from *trusted* sources, and such recovery will often be possible. Any series of refusals may alert one to the possibility that one needs more or better sponsorship; and of course this is particularly important in a situation of intense conflict. Actually, in periods of intense conflict, however, some people are particularly glad to be able to unburden themselves to a discreet outsider—but they need to be assured he really is discreet.

As Roy himself, of course, did, it is also important to remember that the basic purpose is not to get interviews but to collect data relevant to some problem or descriptive of some situation; frequently, the circumstances of the refusal, the way in which it is done, the excuses given, the reaction to the interviewer, may provide valuable data or, at least, hypotheses about the situation. The student on an interviewing assignment, for a research course, for example, and, for that matter, the hired interviewer generally, feels he has to get interviews, come what may; but the teacher or project director should make clear that the interviews are only a means and that other ways of getting relevant data can be equally acceptable means. In order to emphasize this point, it is useful to read not only Roy but Webb, Campbell, Schwartz, and Sechrest, and Lerner's article on "Interviewing Frenchmen."

It is also possible that the project description may, for some reason, seem threatening or that something about the would-be interviewer's appearance, voice, manner, or identification may provoke uneasiness. In general, if the interviewer himself makes a personal effort to get interviews, such reasons for suspiciousness will begin to suggest themselves, and these reasons themselves may often serve as data of interest and utility (as was true in Roy's case, to some extent).

One way to discourage many interviewees or to get shunted off to a specialist is to *explain* in detail what the project is or is supposed to be about. As Whyte tells us, the rather elaborate cover story which he had devised for his *Street Corner Society* study (p. 21)

> proved too elaborate for Cornerville people. I soon found that people were developing their own explanation about me; I was writing a book about Cornerville. This might seem entirely too vague an explanation and yet it sufficed. . . . Whether it was a good thing to write a book about Cornerville depended entirely on people's opinions of me personally. If I was all right, then my project was all right; if I was no good, then no amount of explanation could convince them.

To be sure, elite people, like the prominent businessmen whom Kincaid and Bright wished to interview, are accustomed to much more complex explanations than most of the Cornerville inhabitants in whom Whyte was interested. Nevertheless, elite people, given a *complex* explanation, tend, in my judgment, to feel that the matter probably should be handled by some specialist, or that it is something they do not know anything about, or that it may prove embarrassing. On the latter point they may reason that the interviewers are knowledgeable and informed and no doubt, therefore, will ask complicated questions; and elite people (like nonelite people) generally do not like the idea of being embarrassed by being unable to answer. (I have heard of cases where experienced scholars could not get in to see some distinguished person, and college undergraduates did; I suspect that the college undergraduates made the whole thing seem simple, an enjoyable opportunity for the distinguished person to show off, whereas the experienced scholar frightened the distinguished person with the thought that questions might be asked which might show up the latter's ignorance.) I suspect that Kincaid and Bright may have explained *too much* about their project; apparently, they did tell potential respondents that it dealt with civil defense, a matter in which very few businessmen[2] are interested and which they generally fail to see as relevant or significant. Now, if the explanation had been couched in more general terms—something about what business can do to construct a better national military policy or something about national goals— they would have got more acceptances. Of course, some respondents would have insisted then on talking about national military policy or national goals; many interviewers, perhaps Kincaid and Bright, would have regarded such conversation as sheer "dross," but, analogously, in the trade study I found that introduction-stimulated "dross" (as it seemed to me to begin with) turned out to be extremely valuable, in this way: more and more as the study proceeded, I introduced the project in general terms, about how business and government are related, and did not stress reciprocal trade as such at all. So, many respondents talked about these general matters. But their comments on these points, as it turned out, gave me a much clearer idea of their perspectives than I ever could have got by confining myself to reciprocal trade, and reflection about what was said about these general issues permitted me much better to see what was said about reciprocal trade in terms of the respondents' frames of reference.

The major point here, however, is that refusals will be cut down if one tries to understand why prospective respondents are uncomfortable about promising an interview. For instance, I have found small businessmen much more difficult to see than people in larger businesses; this is because the small restaurant owner, for instance, has to be answering customers, supervising his help, and so forth, and he really cannot quit just because an interviewer is there; nor can he foresee when he may have a rush. Were I again to have to interview restaurant owners, as I did in 1943 on price control matters, I would not simply regard them as less "cooperative" than, say, furniture manufacturers, whom I was also seeing, but try to figure out some mechanism and timing by which I could make it easy for them to see me. (In one neighborhood restaurant-bar, the best time, I discovered accidentally, would have been early in the morning, 1 or 2 A.M. weekdays, when only the regular customers generally stayed on, and when the girls were cleaning up.)

Once a person has refused, however, it is often desirable to get him to reconsider; (one can never be sure how the refusers will differ from the people immediately willing to be interviewed). One example of handling refusers: a congressman's brother and assistant refused to let me see him on the grounds that "since the project was a Massachusetts [Institute of Technology] project there were plenty of Massachusetts congressmen to see," so I got twelve people from his state whom I knew— editors, college professors, businessmen, citizens—to write him, asking that as a personal favor he see me. I got a phone call a few days later from the congressman himself asking me to come down "any time . . . any time at all," and had what turned out to be one of the most illuminating interviews in the entire series. A senator refused to see me on the grounds that "I am being asked to betray my constituents' privacy." (We were asking him, as we said, about what he heard from constituents about business problems.) I had the chancellor of his state university, for which I had done some special work, get in touch with him, explaining that I was a very discreet and responsible person and saying that the university felt the project was entirely worthwhile. So, the senator give me a perfectly satisfactory interview.

Although my colleagues on the trade study did not agree with me (they felt there was an element of threat), I believe that this

kind of approach, if used judiciously, would generally be rewarding. Of course, there should be no element of threat in any
such approach, nor was there; the congressman and the senator
were being asked by constituents to do a favor, and doing favors
is the life-blood of Congress-constituency relationships.

Had I been in Hortense Powdermaker's situation, unable to get
to see the top brass in the movie industry, I would have remembered that big movie companies have (a) Washington representatives who were, in the 1940's, often more sophisticated about
intellectual matters than the executives (Governor Arnall, for
instance, served as a representative of some movie producers in
Washington), and (b) New York attorneys and stockbrokers,
some of whom were academically very aware. I would have got
in touch with some of these people, starting out with those law
firms or stock brokerage firms, where (since she was Jewish)
someone might have the respect that many New York Jews have
for intellectuals and Queens College professors. Probably, this
would have been sufficient; but if it had not been, I would have
explored the following possibilities: (c) there usually were some
political figures in Los Angeles, Sacramento, and Washington,
who had symbiotic relationships with the movie industry—I would
have found out who they were and which ones of them would
be likely to sympathize with an intellectual enterprise of the sort
Powdermaker was engaged in; or (d) if other resources failed
(and I don't think they would have) I would have considered
hiring an agent to get me interviews with the top people; an
experienced Hollywood agent would probably have known how
to circumvent protective assistants and secretaries, what line to
use in selling the executives on seeing me, and so on, and the
sheer brassiness of the idea might have appealed to agents and
businessmen alike!

In general, for reasons stated in Chapter VI and implied in
the quotation from Whyte, above, any use of such contacts should
be, as far as possible, on a favor-giving basis. The intermediary
should not explain the project but ask a favor. This avoids the
danger that the intermediary may try to interpret the project to
the potential respondent and thereby affect the content of the
interview. Time permitting, it would be well, for the same reason

and also to avoid any chance of being tagged as a dependent of so-and-so, to use different intermediaries with different prospective interviewees, rather than just one or two. It would be well to check at the beginning of the interview what the interviewee thinks you are looking for, to try to find out whether he has been given an elaborate explanation by the intermediary.

Somewhat along the same line—it happened to involve chiefly the administration of psychological tests for 6 hours or more (with some survey-type interviewing), but it could as well have been a matter of specialized interviewing—in the Jastak study of the incidence of mental retardation in Delaware, in which it was considered logically necessary to get full responses from all members of certain families randomly chosen from the entire population, I arranged, as a consultant, to employ part-time a woman who had many community contacts throughout that state; she introduced herself in advance to mayors, prominent clergymen, and others, so that when any respondent proved hard to locate or unwilling to participate, she could call these people and ask them to intercede. As a result, there were very few refusals.

One of the most stimulating discussions of how to get an introduction is provided by a writer in a seemingly unrelated field. Altick in "Hunting for Manuscripts" describes many different ways of locating manuscripts and getting introductions to owners who may be reluctant to have them explored. (Lewis's two books provide more detailed accounts of what he calls the "minuet" of acceptance and rejection, which concludes [usually] by the scholar or the collector getting the manuscript.) The significance of these stories is that they show scholars deliberately using influence and knowledge of channels to secure access to needed data. The tradition in interviewing, generally, has been to refrain from any such efforts, partly because it is felt that the interviewee will necessarily give a poor interview if he has been exposed to any "pressure" in trying to get to him. I know of no general evidence to this effect at all; Wax gives an excellent theoretical reason for doubting the general validity of the point, when she explains why some interviewees tell more of significance to people whom they regard as real outsiders or with whom they do not identify than to people with whom they have great rapport, because, for instance, it is easier or even rewarding to tell to outsiders "harsh, bitter" truths, which one would wish to conceal from people one likes.

In fact, the point can only be defended if we can demonstrate that what the interviewee gets out of the interview *demands* that the interviewee have a feeling of complete nonaggressiveness on the part of the interviewer. Nadel, again, shows us one kind of situation where this would not be true; and I suspect that a high proportion of businessmen and politicians in the United States feel more comfortable or stimulated with a little aggression in the background of a superficially polite relationship than they do with a completely "nice" situation.

This does not contradict the point made earlier that one should be "neutral on the interviewee's side." For, to continue a revealing conversation or to go into details, interviewees generally do need to be reassured that the interviewer "understands . . ." which means he must adopt what the interviewee regards as a conceivable and pertinent frame of reference, something which the interviewee shares. Wax could well enough have made a strenuous effort to secure interviews under some circumstances with subjects whom she comments on as follows: "I have heard men . . . relate in detail how they planned to terrorize whole communities and beat up anyone who opposed them, expecting that these acts when published would redound to their credit." But she could not refuse them the credit of taking seriously the moral and self-laudatory justifications which they expressed. The latter refusal would be insulting to the ego, humiliating; the aggressive effort to get an interview would be a kind of gamesmanship, enjoyed by a good many, though not all, people.

What Does the Interviewee Get Out of the Interview?

Of course, basically, the best way to answer the question about how aggressively to try to get interviews depends upon what the interviewee gets out of the interview or out of the contemplation of being interviewed (and of what costs he attributes to it in contemplation). There is practically no material to my knowledge which throws any light at all upon what the interviewee gets out of the contemplation of the interview; Wax in the article just cited suggests that simple curiosity (what are they asking these other people?) may in some cases help to get an interview. And, in a group situation, when some have been interviewed, others will feel, as a few have told me, "When are you going to get around to me?" implying "If not, why not?"

Once an interview has been started, the interviewee must get something out of it, also. Probably, the greatest value which many interviewees receive—the reason why they enjoy the interview—is the opportunity to teach, to tell people something. From this standpoint there is something to be said for an interviewer's looking and seeming young; I judge I got more from some interviewees when I was in my 30's and seemed or looked somewhat younger than my age than I could get from similar interviewees now that I am in my 50's and do not seem younger than most of them. There are, I trust, compensating advantages in age; and, indeed, in some cases, younger people might be persuaded to tell me how things have gone since the time I knew about them.

Many interviewers and investigators have commented upon the pleasure informants and interviewees get out of teaching; it seems to be, for instance, almost a commonplace in anthropological field work that one reason why the anthropologist starts to learn a language is not only that it is, indeed, necessary, but that it gives informants and subjects an opportunity to take the role of teacher. Another value which, seemingly, many interviewees receive out of far-ranging interviews has been commented upon only by Caplow as far as I recollect. His comments conform to observations made by Raymond Bauer and me in the trade study, and can be generalized somewhat further.

People of importance (like people of unimportance) often have no real opportunity to talk to an *understanding* stranger—meaning, by a stranger, someone who will presumably make no claims, no use of the remarks, which will affect the speaker in the future. When a man is talking to his personal assistant, or his wife, or his colleague about his job or his problems, they may understand him very well. But there is always the possibility that something said to these people—a speculation or interpretation—

will annoy or irritate, or will commit the speaker in some way in which he does not want to be committed. Furthermore, conversation with wives, colleagues, personal assistants, about general matters, general considerations, one's own history and development, is often difficult simply because it is intruded upon by practical, immediate considerations, about things which have to be done right now, or which at any rate can well be taken up right now. Yet, a good many people in a specialized position do have some taste for self-analysis, or for discussing the nature of what they do in general terms, or simply for telling people in detail what they have done. Most strangers simply do not know enough, do not know the right vocabulary, interrupt with "stupid" and irrelevant comments, have to have too much explained to them. So, the interviewer who has bothered to "understand," who knows what the interviewee is talking about, whose comments are relevant, but who will not make any future claims, who will not regard himself as having received a commitment, no matter what is said, can indeed provide a pleasurable experience to the interviewee. This is the only explanation I can make as to why interviewees often have been so reluctant to let us go (with congressmen and politicians, very markedly, I sometimes found it difficult to get away even when I felt I had had all I could absorb at one sitting) and why in some cases they appear to have genuinely enjoyed the interview. (There has been a considerable variation in this, not only between different interviewees, which is to be expected, but between different projects for reasons which I do not understand. It seems to me that on the trade study and on my study of Watertown town politics in 1959 more interviewees were really eager to continue than in any other projects I have been engaged in; in the Watertown study, it may have been because so many of the participants in this situation felt the situation was unresolved and unfinished [as indeed it was] and that nobody would really listen to their particular angle.)

As far as I can see, the experiences most analogous to a talk with an understanding interviewer-stranger occurs at professional meetings, where one can talk to someone in a similar situation in another organization to whom one has no future or present obligations. (Although I have never actually tried it, it seems to me speculatively that, because this is one of the reasons people come to professional meetings, maybe in some studies better interviews could be obtained at such association meetings than elsewhere; people would be in the right frame of mind.)

Gusfield has made the most careful attempt of which I know to try to guess at what interviewees on a project got out of the experience. He makes a point which ought to be obvious but which is often overlooked in discussions of how to "handle" interviewees: "The interviewee has to get something out of the interview—*otherwise there is no reason for him to open up*" (emphasis supplied). He found that in an upstate New York Women's Christian Temperance Union group his status as a professor pleased them; they liked working with a professor. They had middle-class notions of status. But in Illinois, where the W.C.T.U. group was lower in class level, and did not value professorial prestige, his status cut no ice. He had, with them, to take the role of someone, working on a thesis, *who needed help* —and evidently these women were of the kind who like (or feel an obligation) to aid a person who needs help.

Whom Should You Try to See First?
And Whom Should You Avoid Seeing First?

One of the important differences between elite and specialized interviewing, on the one hand, and survey interviewing on the other, is that in elite and specialized interviewing it is not usually possible to determine by any mechanical method who should be interviewed. The population cannot be satisfactorily randomized or stratified in advance; and different interviewees make quite different and unequal contributions to the study.

Whom should you see first? Heard, Powdermaker, and Dexter all started out with interviewees and informants whom they thought would be more favorably inclined, more apt to be responsive. This is, in general, a good approach, but one should protect against two possible risks which are involved: (a) The interviewees with whom one starts are more apt to be "one's own kind of people" and to share the preconceptions of the investigator; hence, starting out with them may in fact lead the interviewer to rely too much and too long on unchallenged assumptions which would be more quickly questioned through interviews with others. An example here is the tendency I think I have observed among academics to interview first political figures with the most contacts and good-will in the universities; these politicians in fact also differ from other politicians in a number of other ways. (b) If the interviewer is *visible*, the fact that he sees *first* people of a certain type may have labeled him as "on their side" before he gets to others. For example, in a faction-ridden state government department, it is entirely possible that the interviewer may have been observed going into the offices of so-and-so and such-and-such long before he gets around to their opponents; but in the United States Congress, most congressmen and senators are sufficiently absorbed in other matters so that they are unlikely to have seen or heard anything about whom a given interviewer has seen previously.

Generally speaking, an interviewer or investigator will start a project by looking for introductions and references from those who have or have had contact with an organization, situation, or institution. Such persons will normally be asked for suggestions as to whom to see first. *It is important to remember that their unchallenged responses may very often be seriously misleading, wasteful, and time-consuming.*

Perhaps, the worst thing that can happen is to be referred to some interviewee who *insists* on taking the investigator under his wing and adopting him as a protégé, *but* who is evidently regarded as an enemy, a bore, or a has-been by important people in the community or organization. Often, further questioning of one's starting points will indicate that a person who is suggested may be dangerous for such reasons. But, in any case, three precautions are usually wise: (a) The interviewer should always make clear that he is going to see a number of other people, and (b) that his first interviews are merely preliminary. (c) *At this stage*, he should not let the people from whom he has got references—or any one else, no matter how kind-hearted or well-intentioned or academically well-known—write or phone or personally introduce him, because then he may find himself saddled with an incubus. In 1937, when I was a very inexperienced field worker, for example, one factor in leading me to give up a projected study was discomfort with a situation where a union executive, who had been shunted to one side by the real powers in the union and was, evidently, disliked by many colleagues, threatened to adopt me as a protégé; I did not, at that time, have any idea how to handle the situation. At best, such things will always be difficult.

And there are other dangers in taking referrals at face value, without cross-questioning one's preliminary contacts. Very often, the people one is referred to are simply people whom the contact likes, but who, in fact, know nothing or next-to-nothing about the situation; they may live in a community or hold office in an organization but not be particularly observant or involved. Or the contact may refer one to people who are really significant, but it is hardly ever desirable to start out one's interviews with the most important people in an organization. Although, conceivably, some particular hypothesis might be tested by such a procedure, such people are far less likely to be responsive to a relatively naive interviewer than to one who has gathered some knowledge about the situation; and obviously, after one has conducted a number of interviews, one will be and appear less naive. Also, early interviews often require one to ask for a good deal of factual information, which a number of people can supply, and there is no point in wasting the time of a top man on such matters and perhaps shutting off the possibility of later interviews with him. This is a difficult point to make to kind-hearted people; I suppose on a dozen occasions I have had to say more or less firmly, "No, I would rather not see so-and-so to begin with; he's too important for me, now." It is also frequently true, finally, that people at the head of an organization know little about the details of its working.

It is possible to be much more definite about whom NOT to start out with than about whom to see first.

It is likely, even at best, that one's first few interviews will be with people who prove relatively nonproductive. But questioning referrals and questioning each interviewee as to whom to see and why will increase the likelihood of getting to people who can provide one with really useful information. Where I think it safe to do so, I explain that I want intelligent, judicious people who know the way things are really done, not just the way they are supposed to be done, who have been around for long enough to have some sense of the history of the situation or organization, and (if I can make the point clear) who like to think in comparative and abstract terms.

A good deal can be learned by asking early interviewees whom one should see later—this not only suggests whom one ought to see, but it also teaches one about personal interrelationships in a situation. One warning that can be disregarded, so far as my experience goes, is this: It is very frequent for an interviewee to say "I think you should see so-and-so, if he'd talk; but I don't think he will." Often, he does.

In addition to the person who has been around for a long time, there is one other kind of person who may be somewhat responsive and able to discuss a situation. That is someone who has been in the organization or community for six months or a year and has come from some similar organization or community, so that he or she can make comparisons. The key question(s), in whatever form, to such people are: "Supposing somebody else with your practical, relevant experience and background were coming here, what would you think he should be told about: (a) things here which are different from what he would expect, (b) things which he might expect to be different which are just the same?" Or, "What do you wish somebody had told you?"

Outlook and temperament are far more important than position for most elite and specialized interviewing, of course; in a set of "exploratory interviews" in various states, the most successful and rewarding interview, by far, I had in one state was with a state librarian; in another state an officer of the budget agency was most helpful; in a third an administrative analyst at the state university; in a fourth an officer of the legislative research council. But, I have talked with other state librarians who were just technical librarians, other state budget officers who were just bookkeepers, other administrative analysts at state universities who were just concerned with administration in a narrow sense. Nevertheless, in regard to any organization or situation it might be a good, preliminary practice to list the *kinds* of positions in which people might be likely to come in contact with and observe what one is interested in, and then interview people in these posts to begin with, granted they are not too important or inaccessible, As a matter of fact, in many organizational and community studies, what such people do *not* know, do not come in contact with, do not regard as part of their job, may also be important.

Whom Do You See Later?
How Do You Select Further Interviewees?

I have put the phrase "exploratory interviews," above, in quotes; actually, "preliminary interview" would be a better phrase, but exploratory has become a common term in social science research. Actually, *all* interviews in elite or specialized interviewing are, or should be, *exploratory*, from beginning to end. It was, for instance, fairly late in the trade study that I discovered that interviews in the cork-processing industry might supply us with information which we did not have; and so I arranged for such interviews. The interview which suggested this area for investigation was, therefore, "exploratory"; and so, in fact, were interviews, conducted primarily on other topics, after the field work was formally completed, which suggested to me points I should take account of in the write-up.

Field research, that is, always ought to be and frequently is a process of continuing discovery. One is learning how to re-formulate or at least modify one's formulation of a problem; one is locating new data.[3] So, the decision as to whom to see depends largely upon one's on-going reflection about the issues, upon new data and hypotheses that come to one's attention, from whatever source—often from earlier interviews. Of course, practical considerations or serendipity play a part; the accident of being asked to give a speech in a particular community led me to think of interviewing a toy manufacturer in that town (in order to get the trade project to cover the expenses of my trip) and it turned out that was an especially helpful interview.

I have found it useful when interviewees speak of or even hint at views and aspects which they are opposed to or do not understand on an issue to ask for specific names of individuals who express such views—or, of course, who engage in disapproved-of actions (as, for example, people who engage in "illegitimate pressure"). My interview reports, therefore, contain names of many people, most of whom it has been impractical to follow up, but I have by this approach learned of many people worth seeing, whom I did see and from whom I learned a good deal. Of course, it is also useful to ask for suggestions about people who express approved views or engage in approved actions; but the interviewee is more likely spontaneously to suggest that one see such people.

On Actually Arranging for the Interview

One of the points on which interviewers seem to differ a good deal is how they try to arrange an interview in advance. Heard, for instance, reports that in 227 interviews (45 per cent of his total) with southern politicians he simply walked in, introduced himself, and held the interview forthwith. One wonders a bit whether an interviewer making a study of university executives could simply barge in on Alexander Heard, now that he has become chancellor of Vanderbilt University, and hold the interview forthwith! It was certainly true that southern politicians of the old school always seemed to have more leisure for a chat than most influential people in the United States or Canada; and they were far more courteous and accessible to unintroduced strangers than many such persons. Heard argues that his procedure saved the interviewer the bother of an explanation (which is true) and quite a bit of time; again, now that there are jet airliners and influential people are always making appointments out of town, it is probably more necessary to pin them down to a specific time and place. However, it would still be feasible to phone the prospective interviewee from a headquarters and say that one is planning to be in town and can one see him that afternoon. I know of some interviewers who assert that this is the best way to do things. There still appear to be enough people around who are impressed by long-distance calls so that such calls have some weight.

I myself have always felt that a phone call giving the interviewee a choice of a number of times is preferable, and smacks less of needless pressure. Where I actually am going to be in a community for only a few days, or some other factor makes it desirable to get an interview soon, I try to explain the factors in my own schedule, but I always try to make clear that, so far as possible, I will be at the interviewee's disposal as to time. I often do tell the interviewee or his secretary that I am trying to see some other people during the week and I hope he will not mind if things happen so that I call up and see if some change in time would do; of course, whether I say this depends upon the nature of the conversation at the beginning.

For the trade study, I had a statement mimeographed explaining the nature of the sponsorship and study in very general terms, and then a week or two before I wanted to see someone, I enclosed this with a covering letter, stating when I wanted to see the man and about when I would call his office. I have more often relied only on telephone calls, recently, but this has been chiefly due to laziness about writing avoidable letters; I think the written notice was on the whole desirable—secretaries often had the letter out on their desk on the day I called and no further explanation was needed about the project or me. (However, in the study of the effectiveness of detail men and medical advertising, my hunch is that a preliminary letter would have hardened the resolution of more physicians not to be bothered by such an inquiry; it is possible that Kincaid and Bright's letter about their civil-defense study might have had led to the same sort of reaction; the hypothesis here is that a letter in advance is not desirable if it suggests that the project will deal with something that prospective interviewees might find presumptuous, boring, or distasteful.)

When I have made brief out-of-town trips to interview, I have written to a few people in the city to which I am going, asking for appointments the first day I am going to be there. I find I have recently made one natural mistake; in order to avoid having no appointments or in case some initial interviewee turns out to be quite wasteful and hardly worth recording, I have tended to overschedule myself the first day—which in fact is a bad mistake, because I get behind in writing up interviews, and/ or may be too tired the second day. In general, in the future I will place more effort in starting the first day or two with people who may have documents which I should read, company historians, state librarians, etc.

Personally, I find the most irritating and annoying aspect of interviewing is calling up to ask for an interview. I have, therefore, on several occasions hired some one to make these calls for me. This has an additional advantage—where it is useful, the caller can, if necessary, say a little more about me, on my behalf, of a favorable nature, than I can well say myself. However, I know that in one instance this was distinctly overdone and could have frightened off some prospective interviewees, so hired callers should be warned against overdoing it. Of course, if one knows someone who can be trusted to make such calls discreetly, and who is not identified with some particular faction or group in a city to which one has not previously gone, and one can spend only a brief period of time there, it is helpful to have appointments scheduled in advance—among other things, to find out if there is something about the particular time one has chosen which makes it particularly bad for the trip.

There is one advantage in making the calls oneself, much as I dislike to do so. The way in which the man or his secretary explains or comments, the people one may be referred to (and it often happens that for quite legitimate reasons, one is referred to somebody else in an organization or agency), and so on— things of this sort provide data which a hired clerk can hardly be expected to recognize. On the other hand, if one is asking somebody who does have some understanding of the project to do the calling, it is likely that such a person will overexplain, telling the interviewees too much about what (he thinks) the project is and therefore prejudicing the interviewee's answers.

One should accept any time the interviewee proposes, if at all possible. Place is a trickier matter. In general, a man's private office is best, although the most instructive single interview I ever had was with a senator who came to see me in my hotel room. In general, when a man invites you to meet him at home it is desirable to try to see if it can be shifted to his office, because some interviewees will let their families come in and out freely, and generally will tolerate interruptions which they would not in their offices. Of the twenty or so interviews I have held where a man's family was present, I can only think of one where this was not a distraction and a bother (in those cases where family members are actually professional colleagues, the situation is different). If you have any reason to suspect a man does not have a private office, it may be well to see if a cup of coffee or a drink can be proposed. But a cup of coffee or a drink should only be taken in some place where one can be fairly sure of having privacy; to be joined by others is likely to be upsetting unless one has planned for them.

Of course, it is obvious that the foregoing refers to the typical, professional or quasi-professional man in English-speaking North America or Western Europe. There are many places and many groups in the United States, for that matter, where there will be difficulty in getting a room of one's own in which to talk. Dollard in his study of Negroes in a southern town found it useful to rent an office in a downtown building, used by other professional men, so they could come and talk with him freely and privately; other similar devices may be necessary with one or another category of specialized interviewee in this country. Of course, much that is said here would be inapplicable or impractical in some other society. It may well be, as some anthropologists tell us (see Paul), that under some circumstances interviews with several persons can be as rewarding as or more rewarding than with one person. It is quite probable, as S. L. A. Marshall reports (pp. 16-17), that in reconstructing a military action it is better to have as many participants as possible present, and it may well be there are other occasions in our own society where several interviewees are preferable to one. But I would think under all circumstances where only one interview is involved that the interview should be restricted to persons prepared to comment *relevantly*, closed to those who will constitute a *distraction*, and that the interviewer should be prepared for the people he will interview. Of course, where there are a series of interviews, one may alter the conditions between one interview and another in the series with great profit. (Such variation is particularly likely to be helpful with persons who are genuine informants.)

One other kind of situation where the interview ought not to be in a private office or hotel room should be mentioned. As Kenneth Burke (p. 446) says, "the situation remembers, not the man" or, more prosaically put, the immediate environment determines the roles people assume and consequently what they remember, and also most people are reminded by logically irrelevant sights, sounds, and smells, of events and attitudes they otherwise would forget. For certain studies, therefore, or with certain interviewees, it is worth having the interview somewhere else, not in a private office. Despite the psychoanalytic tradition of the private room, some of Dollard's interviewees might have remembered more, and more vividly, about their earlier life-histories if they had been walking with him up and down the fields where events had taken place (of course, in his case such strolls would have been unwise). In interviewing some state legislators, it might be that they are more likely to assume the legislative role and give a legislative-type answer in the legislative corridors or the hotel or restaurant next to the capitol than they are in their private business offices. But the possibility of such gains does not in general justify losing privacy; there has to be some very specific reason for believing the risk is worthwhile in terms of particular data to be gathered or particular interviewees to be seen.

In general, with most interviewees, lunch is a mistake. If one is eating, one can not take notes very well (I suspect that running a tape recorder is still more difficult against lunch-time noise). And most people tend to make general conversation much more at lunch-time than in an office. But a lunch in a place where other people known to either interviewer or interviewee may feel free to interrupt is not only a mistake, it is often very detrimental.

However, an invitation to lunch *after* an interview is "completed" is a very different matter; one can often check matters from a different vantage point and the interviewee will think back to some of the things he said and "correct" them. Or, if joined by others, he will explain to them what you are about and ask their comments.

Lacking a private office, a conference room or a hotel room— any place where interruptions can be controlled—will do. On the principle of controlling interruptions, when both interviewer and interviewee are in hotels in a strange city, it is better to have the interview in the interviewer's hotel room if it is not too unimpressive.

Naturally, one of the most frequent questions asked is: "How long do you want?" I answer this by saying: "That depends very much on you (or your boss). Different people find it interesting to talk about the subject in more or less detail. In general, I find that it takes" and then, if pushed further to estimate the time, I specify a time a little, but not much, less than the normal time which interviews on the particular project take. For instance, on the trade study, interviews with congressmen seemed ordinarily to run about forty-five minutes; so I generally indicated I hoped the prospective interviews could take thirty-five.

In soliciting an interview, it is helpful to bear in mind the point which will be explained further below—use some general phrase which the interviewee can interpret for himself. *Do not be any more precise than you absolutely have to be about what you are looking for.* By the same token, I have never been willing to give examples of questions (still less a written list); although such lists have been requested of me, occasionally, I have never had the request made an issue (however, I have heard of cases where this has been done; I would consider this a refusal and handle it as such).

And, for the reasons mentioned above in connection with refusals, overexplanation or overstress on one's own prestige and knowledge or even the expertise of the sponsoring organization may well set a bad background for the interview itself. It is occasionally the case that a project director or sponsoring organization, without experience in field interviewing, wants to give an elaborate explanation of what he is looking for in a letter of introduction; whenever the objective is genuine exploration— to find out how interviewees look at things and put things together—such letters should be resisted. They may do well enough where one is testing a hypothesis. And they may be necessary in asking respondents to answer a written questionnaire; but the great advantage of the elite and specialized interview technique is that the interviewer can adapt his comments and questions to the unfolding interaction between himself and the interviewee. This advantage should not be thrown away.

On Introducing Yourself and Starting the Interview

It can never be assumed that the interviewee remembers who you are or what your project is; indeed, in a couple of cases when an interview was interrupted by an emergency and resumed a couple of weeks later, I found that I made a mistake by starting off without explaining all over again who I was and who sponsored me! It is important to explain at the beginning of each interview and, for that matter, each interview session, who you are, what the sponsorship is, and, to the necessary degree, what the project is about.

A good many interviewees will want to know the sponsorship and it is important that this be statable in a fairly clear fashion. (There are noticeable differences between different groups here; a number of businessmen and congressmen wanted to know what the Center for International Studies at M.I.T. was and who financed the trade study, whereas no physician, that I recollect, inquired what the Mendota Research Associates were.) The sheer complexity of some sponsorships is at least a minor disadvantage; to explain the whole thing sounds confusing, yet some suspicious or legalistically minded interviewees will want to know exactly who each sponsor is. In letters of introduction, it is therefore of some value to simplify statements about sponsorships and direction, as far as this can possibly be done. Some interviewees may ask who is financing a project.[4] If this information is complicated, it might be desirable to try to have it available in writing in as simple a form as possible—only to be shown to those interviewees who ask.

Intuitively, and without any direct evidence, I would be inclined to suppose that it would be marginally helpful at every stage of getting and introducing an interview to apply the approach of Elmo Wheeler's *Tested Sentences That Sell*, and other studies of point-of-contact salesmanship. It is probable that some *names* sound much better to a given class of hoped-for respondents than another—for instance, if I were trying to interview executives of the John Birch Society, I would suppose it would sound better to come from an Urban Studies Institute than from a Center for International Studies, and it would certainly be better to emphasize financing from, for example, a Rheem Foundation than from a Rockefeller Foundation.[5] Similarly, readers will be able to think of names with positive and negative affect on leaders of black people's movements or the new left. To a lesser extent, I suspect the same sort of concern affects other types of groups; in interviewing civil defense and safety officials, I found Oak Ridge National Laboratory to be a plus sponsor, but there may well be planning officials to whom Oak Ridge National Laboratory creates a minor negative reaction, because of distaste for atomic warfare.

Of course, one can not ordinarily change the names of sponsors; but it is possible to change the order in which they are named, if there are several, and to emphasize or minimize or occasionally change the names of centers, committees, or other subgroups. In talking with persons whom I suspected of opposing reciprocal trade extension, I down-played the title "Center for International Studies" and simply talked about Massachusetts Institute of Technology. It might have been possible, had it been worth the bother, to give some particularly reassuring title to our particular study. And, indeed, if a given sponsorship involves the use of a name that put some potential interviewees off, it might be feasible to add some other organization, more attractive to them, as co-sponsor.

Interviewees very often ask the interviewer a good many questions about himself or sometimes about the project supervisor. Although this is partly simply a conversational breaking of the ice, it is often designed to find out whether the interviewer is the sort of person the interviewee wants to talk freely to. On the whole, my impression is that a rough line of distinction can be drawn between (a) professional-cosmopolitans whose questions are directed towards the interviewer's training and capacity, relationship with the sponsoring organization, etc., and (b) personalistic-locals who are more concerned with the nonprofessional aspects of an interviewer's life. It is my impression that in the past 20 years there has been a considerable increase in the proportion of professional-cosmopolitans in American elite positions. Naturally, there are many mixed types.

Time can be saved, to the degree that people are interested in one's professional qualifications and knowledge of their professions by duplicating an experience statement about oneself which one can offer to show the interviewee as a personal introduction; naturally, such a statement should indicate something about one's knowledge of the kinds of matters one will raise with a given set of interviewees. In my most recent interviews, dealing with state and provincial government, I usually mention that the most relevant thing may be my own practical experience in Massachusetts state government and the fact that I have already talked with officials in a good many states and provinces about similar problems. I also have carried with me, simply because it looks more impressive than a mimeographed statement, a jacket of one of my books (which, since it has a picture, confirms that I am who I say I am). My impression is that such a professional emphasis tends to reduce the time spent on usually pointless personal questions (Are you related to this particular Dexter whom the interviewee knew at such-and-such a place?)— pointless for the kind of interview I characteristically conduct.

Of course, there are projects and interviewees where the personal note must be struck. To give a contrast; although I am a distant relative of the late Senator Green of Rhode Island, it did not seem to me worthwhile in interviewing him to mention the matter; it seemed obvious that he would be (as indeed he was) willing to teach me in a professional manner. On the other hand, the late Senator Malone of Nevada cross-questioned me for some thirty-five minutes about my background; and the thing that, seemingly, finally decided him to "open up" was my statement that my grandfather had been a Baptist minister. More generally, there are far more state legislators than congressmen, I suspect, with whom it would be worthwhile to establish some tie of mutual acquaintance, schooling, athletic interest, and the like.

In general, however, my feeling is that if the interview goes at all well, it is best to omit any mention of personal factors, substantively irrelevant to the interview, unless it is quite clear that the interviewee is personalistically oriented. Otherwise, one may (a) waste time in trying to establish confidence which can be better established by the substance of the discussion, and (b) run at least a slight risk that one may lead the interviewee to address himself to your mutual acquaintances as well as to you. Riesman points out (p. 574) that many of the interviewees in the Lazarsfeld and Thielens study of attitudes on academic freedom were addressing themselves past the interviewers to Lazarsfeld himself. This was not in that case harmful, but in interviewing a particular United States senator who had been a student of my grandfather's and may have remembered him clearly, I saw no value in mentioning the fact, because it might lead him to talk to me as though my political and ethical views were those of my grandfather. Such personalistic contacts should, of course, be mentioned, if this can be done without pretentiousness, if the interview is limping badly; and they may be worth mentioning at the end of the interview, in any event, in order to see if they lead the interviewee to feel he should add something.

Although they will rarely be needed, extreme embarrassment may be avoided if one has on one's person at all times credentials which show quite clearly: (a) that one is who one says one is, and (b) that the project in which one is engaged is quite bona fide. (For example, I have, when engaged in interviewing under a Social Science Research Council grant, had available a report of that body, which shows its responsibility.) It happens so rarely it is easy to forget to take credentials with one; but on the Grodzins project, where all my arrangements had been made orally, I subcontracted a few interviews to a friend who has special competences. In the course of his interviewing in a security agency, some official saw fit to raise the question of his sponsorship and responsibility; at that time, Grodzins was out of Chicago and I was also not available. Once, when I had forgotten to bring even a wallet with me, I was interviewing Pentagon officials, who, hot in their zeal to show me how dreadfully evil the behavior of one of the other services was, were insisting on my reading documents stamped TOP SECRET (despite my protests that I was not cleared and had no official "need to know.") They left me alone with the documents for a few minutes, for some reason; I prayed that no one else would walk in!

In actually starting off the interview, it is often helpful to comment on something in the office which is relevant and shows a man's concerns. Or if one is lucky, one may have heard or overheard while waiting in the outer office, for instance, something which suggests a remark which is likely to be pertinent to what a man is thinking about currently. As a matter of fact, some interviewees more or less rehearse the high points of what they said to their most recent interlocutor of importance, just because it is occupying their mind at the moment; frequently, such a rehearsal serves to provide a lead-in to one's own concerns, and in any case the more an interview is made to seem like a continuation of what a man has just been talking about or concerning himself with, the better the prospect of his opening up quickly.

One mistake which I have made on a number of occasions is to try to carry on an interview in an environment unsuited for it. A legislator who is standing outside the legislative chamber, while half his attention is focused on buttonholing colleagues is not a good subject for an interview; though one might learn something from observing him. I do not know whether, if confronted with such a situation again, I would have the nerve to say in effect, "I need your full attention . . ." but I hope I would ask whether I can arrange some time when he is less preoccupied. The most common difficulty is a man who really lacks a private office; for instance, state legislators or an executive assistant whose room is used as a passageway to his chief's. In all such cases, I shall in the future ask if there is a conference room or if we can have a cup of coffee, or, if worst comes to worst, even meet for a lunch.

Many interviewees stop phone calls for any visitor; actually, however, if there is a choice, I would seriously urge them not to cut off important calls for two reasons: (a) calls give me a break to catch up on my notes, and (b) calls may give a clearer picture of the kind of man I am talking with.

On the Importance of Multi-Interpretable Comments or Questions

In most political interviews, certainly, and I think in most interviews where the important thing is the discovery of a social pattern or value of any sort, it is important to start off with comments or ask questions where the key words are quite vague and ambiguous, so the interviewee can interpret them in his own terms, and out of his own experience. A good example of such a question (though by no means the ideal question to start with!) is the classic "What's this I hear about the trouble in this organization?"

Ordinarily, the questions should be of this nature: "What do you hear from business?" (to congressmen), "What are they worrying you about?" *not* "Do you hear from them about the tariff?" Even better may be, "What people do you hear from most?" "Does anybody pressure you?" Similarly, on the Grodzins project, not "How about the grants your agency is supposed to get from such-and-such a federal department," but "In what ways are you most affected in your work by national matters . . ." and if someone starts telling you, as an official of a racing commission told me, about ex-FBI agents who are employed by some national authority, well and good, you have learned to redefine the impact of the federal government! A question which sharply defines a particular area for discussion is far more likely to result in omission of some vital data which you, the interviewer, have not even thought of. Of course, by this process, your answers are not strictly comparable with one another in terms of a narrow conception of what is factual; but you discover how your interviewees and informants see the issues.

It depends very much what the focus of the study is and how

it is developing how far you raise quite specific issues later on. In the trade study, as it happened, I found my focus was becoming the congressman's conception of his job, the businessman's conceptions of political channels, so throughout the greater part of most interviews I used multi-interpretable questions or comments. On the other hand, in the Grodzins study there were certain factual matters about the influence of federal funds on state procedures which could be asked about quite specifically.

Discussion Rather Than Rat-A-Tat-Tat Questioning

The heading almost speaks for itself. It is my experience and impression—but it may reflect an idiosyncrasy of my own—that many elite interviewees dislike a steady flow of questions (I think this is why some of them dislike press conferences). They would prefer a discussion, or still more, perhaps, something which sounds like a discussion but is really a quasi-monologue stimulated by understanding comments. Often, at any rate, I try to handle the relationship as discussion—two reflective men trying to find out how things happen, but the less informed and experienced one (the interviewer) deferring to the wiser one and learning from him.

Note-Making and Writing Up Notes

There is wide variation between interviewers as to how to take notes. The one rule which is universally agreed to is that notes should be written up as soon as possible after an interview is completed. Powdermaker tells of stopping her car in Indianola at the earliest possible moment after she got away from the interviewee; I often stop for an unnecessary cup of coffee immediately after the interview if there is no other convenient place for me to amplify and clarify the notes I took during it.

Some interviewees believe no notes should be taken during the interview; whatever is the case in other societies or social groups, most United States elite interviewees expect notes to be taken and I have never observed any who appeared to object (except at lunch-time or in the case of unanticipated interviews on predominantly social occasions, both of which seem to me eminently reasonable situations for objection). To be sure, particularly in the trade study and in the Garceau study of business-in-politics, a number of interviewees at some point would say "Now, this is off the record," at which point it is well to stop recording. (Usually a few hasty abbreviations made later can remind you of what was said "off the record.") I have had interviewees ask me to keep opinions which sounded utterly innocuous off the record and then tell me *without* any such insistence of clearly illegal acts or express views "on the record" which could have been used to crucify them if reported in the media.

In fact, one way for the interviewer to exert some control over the interview and to respond without breaking into a valuable monologue is simply by the way he takes notes. Rapid recording, plus a look of interest, is an encouragement; dropping the pencil altogether shows that the interviewee is off the point.

Other interviewers speak of themselves as having taken "verbatim" notes—such phrases even occur in print. This may be true, but seems to me impossible, in general, considering the speed with which many interviewees speak and the number of unfamiliar conceptions they introduce.

My notes taken during the interview rely heavily upon abbreviations and shorthand symbols. I strive particularly to get the *nuances* and turns of phrase which indicate *orientation* and *relationship*. Substance is easier to reconstruct afterwards, but unless these turns of phrase are noted on the wing, they are often lost forever. For some studies, e.g. the study of what is regarded as "political pressure," or for getting clues as to factional conflict within an administrative bureaucracy, these turns of phrase are the key data.

Then, as soon as possible after the interview (or in any breathers provided by phone calls to the interviewee, etc.) I fill in and elaborate these handwritten notes. Then, preferably the same day, I write up the interviews on the typewriter with at least three carbons. I try to report in a somewhat standardized form for any set of interviews (a) what the "interesting" points are that the interview suggested about the project as I conceive it, (b) any particularly interesting ideas or problems of academic interest suggested by the interview but not related to the project (sometimes these turn out later to be relatable), (c) an evaluation and description of the interviewee (and in the future, for reasons suggested in Chapter VI, I shall try to add specific hunches about his attitude towards being interviewed by me), and (d) a note on individuals or types of persons suggested by this particular interview whom it might be worth interviewing later on.

Sidney and Beatrice Webb (p. 83) say: "A highly elaborated and skilled process of 'making notes' besides its obvious utility in recording observations which would otherwise be forgotten is, in sociology, actually an instrument of discovery." They then proceed to describe a system of recording each note on a separate card (the best technique, perhaps unknown in their day, would probably involve 3 x 5 or 4 x 6 pieces of paper with different colored carbons), so that the notes can be shuffled and studied in different combinations. I have never actually known anybody who handled notes on interviews in this fashion to my knowledge; nor was I able to get a great deal of value out of the content-analysis which was done under Ithiel Pool's direction of our interviews on the trade study. However, I am sufficiently convinced by the Webbs so that I suspect their system is worth trying; the only thing is I am not sure that I (or most elite interviewers) really have the patience necessary for their technique.

One other point about making notes: the Webbs are insistent, as in their day was natural, upon the importance of a clear, readable handwriting for the social investigator. If the investigator, nowadays, can read his own handwriting, this is sufficient, but it is absolutely essential that he be a rapid typist; no one should be employed as an elite interviewer who is unable to type up his own notes with carbons, quickly and usably. Transcription by or dictation to paid typists is too costly, handwriting too slow. It is desirable to use an electric portable typewriter (after typing on a standard model for forty-four years, I was able to shift to an electric one and type better and more quickly after only a week's practice). It is true that electric portables are much heavier; but dealers will supply, though they do not push, a carrying case with foam rubber protections so that the machine can be shipped quite safely.

How about a Tape Recorder?

In the course of writing this book, I have changed my mind about the use of a tape recorder. I used to regard it as a nuisance and hardly ever worth the expense. However, I am now sure that a tape-recording of an interview does permit the interviewer to capture nuances of the sort mentioned in the preceding sections. Even more important, along the lines discussed in Chapter VI, listening to a tape-recorded interview will permit a much closer analysis of interviewer-interviewee interaction. Even the best interviewer, as far as I know, though he may get full notes on everything significant said by the interviewee, is not able at the same time to describe how he sounds to the interviewee, or note variations in his own emphasis and approach. But he could get this sort of thing from a tape-recorded interview. And, in the course of time, other people may listen to interviews and note things which a given interviewer takes for granted about himself.

The big item of cost where tape recording is used has been transcription. Bucher, Fritz, and Quarantelli report that transcription and checking take over *nine* hours for every *one* hour of interview time (p. 363, *ASR*)—Professor Quarantelli in a letter to me of November 29, 1968, on the basis of directing the transcription of 2500 recorded interviews on a subsequent project, says: "My impression is that generally [the same ratio] holds true."

Obviously, most projects can not afford such costs; nor would they be worth it. What I suspect may often be worth it (though I have not encountered this particular tactic in practice) would be tape recording of *some* interviews, particularly early, preliminary interviews, followed by the interviewer's listening to them himself, and writing them up, just as he would have done anyway. It might be good practice to write up interviews on the basis of notes, and then see what a tape recording adds for a revised write-up. Of course, it would also be valuable, to have one interviewer write up a project on the basis of notes, and then to have a colleague on the same project write up the same interview on the basis of the tape recording. This would be much less expensive than transcription by secretaries and would have considerable instructive value for the interviewers. According to Bucher, Fritz, and Quarantelli (p. 360, *ASR*), the recorder "readily exposes the extent to which the interview data are influenced by the tactics and verbal activity of the interviewer— something which is very difficult to assess in written interviews." Bucher, Fritz, and Quarantelli (p. 360, *ASR*) point out what seems to them a partially offsetting saving: "Other things being equal, the interviewer who uses a tape recorder is able to obtain more interviews during a given time period." In their particular project, where they were trying to capture and record on the run accounts of disasters while still fresh in people's minds, this was important; but, generally, it is more important that the interviewer should write up his own interview report, so that he reflects about it and carries over that reflection to the next interview.

For research *on* the interview itself (as Richardson, Dohrenwend, and Klein ably demonstrate) tape recording is absolutely indispensable. For demonstration purposes, in classes in methods and the like, tape-recorded interviews are highly desirable. (Of course, for both purposes, videotaping would be even better, but much more expensive, cumbersome, and possibly intrusive).

In the field of oral history, tape recordings seem to be regarded by many practitioners as absolutely essential. Philip C. Brooks, director of the Harry S. Truman Library, for instance, says: "Now, I think that a tape recorder is important enough to oral history to constitute almost a part of the definition," (Dixon and Mink, p. 7; but see Starr's comments on this general point, *ibid*, pp. 22 ff.). There is no doubt that people in other fields who want to learn about the problems of tape recording should consult directors of oral history programs; but the notion which some oral historians seem to have that the tape recorder necessarily makes something more authentic or objective needs a good deal of critical scrutiny, in terms of the transactional theory of interviewing developed in Chapter VI below.

What Makes a Good Interviewer?

A good interviewer has, obviously, as many of the virtues as possible of a good social scientist, a good reporter, and a good listener. There is no point in discussing these virtues in general here.[6]

There are, however, some characteristics which must be especially well developed in the interviewer—which ought to be true of most sorts of interviewers, whether social scientists, physicians, journalists, or social workers. As Sidney and Beatrice Webb say:

> The first, indispensable factor in successful investigation or fruitful observation . . . is an efficient attention. . . . Few (for instance even in listening to lectures) seem to "take in" more than a small proportion of the statements made by the lecturer or even to absorb . . . the points he has most strenuously endeavored to drive home. To quote, "people hear some isolated point and instead of listening to the sentences that follow it, they proceed to build upon it *some notion of their own* of what the speaker is trying to say; and *this notion is what they attend to*, finding a confirmation of it in any fragments which reach their minds afterwards. In fact, they theorise, instead of trying to experience; and usually their theory is based on their own experience, not on the (presently hearable) facts so that from all speaking, *they get only what they have brought to it*, and this is not what the speaker said."
>
> . . . Indeed, most people without being aware of it would much rather retain their own conclusions than learn anything contrary to them. . . . To be a good listener, you need to hear what others have to say. . . .

This bromidic statement is nevertheless crucial; to be able to hear, I have found it helps to put myself in a frame of mind so that I am excited about what I may hear—I can then listen to what would otherwise seem to me boring or platitudinous remarks with concentrated attention and excitement. "There is," in fact, add the Webbs, "a 'moral defect' at the root of the failure of most beginners to achieve discoveries." (That is, they set out to fit what they hear into preconceived patterns.) "The successful investigator is he who is eager to have conventional classifications upset and the orthodox categories transcended. He has in mind the axiom fathered on Heraclitus 'If ye expect not the unexpected, ye shall not find truth.'"

Incidentally, *concentrated attention* is one of the rewards which many interviewees, I infer, get from the interview. Very few people ever receive the flattery of concentrated attention (except possibly from a lover). Concentrated attention involves a second characteristic particularly important for the interviewer. He must be able to shift gears rapidly; that is to say, when the interviewee makes what seems to him to be a jump, he must not show any feeling that there is an irrelevance, but must with one corner of his mind, note that he may need to discover how the interviewee makes the transition, while with the forefront of his attention, he is listening eagerly to what seems to be the new topic. (I may add that one reason why I personally find it much easier to interview one person at a time than to interview several is that I find it too confusing and tiring to pay concentrated attention to several people at a time and to shift gears with each one of them.)

Shifting gears becomes much easier if you are paying concentrated attention because you note cues, implications, and hints which at an ordinary level of involvement would escape you, and so you make a transition with the interviewee. Shifting gears is easier, too, if one avoids another attitude discussed by the Webbs, that of "the false start of a question to be answered . . ." (pp. 34-41). "The very terms in which the question is couched exclude answers of some kinds about which we have not been thinking." This approach is very similar to that argued for by Glaser and Strauss, and means concentrating on the field data (in this case the interviewee), rather than insisting on testing a hypothesis or getting a fact which seems irrelevant to the latter.

A third skill of particular importance to the interviewer is what is described by the Webbs as *empathic understanding* (pp. 47-49). Put in terms currently more fashionable among social scientists, Sjoberg and Nett say (p. 180), "It is the scientist-observer whose conceptual system [whose value, idea, or belief system] lacks closure who is most sensitive to new ideas and patterns of action." One kind of openness is simply the ability to grasp what the other person is experiencing, to feel some of what he feels, to share to some extent his view of his experiences. Although I was not aware of it at the time I published the article, this is part of what I was unconsciously advocating in my 1956 article, "Role Relationships and Conceptions of Neutrality in Interviewing," referred to earlier in this chapter. But there is no necessary contradiction between the kind of sympathetic neutrality I was describing and Nadel's bullying technique, also referred to earlier in the chapter. For it is perfectly possible to challenge, to cross-question, to bully, while *empathizing;* and conversely, it is perfectly possible to be extremely courteous and bland and use the other person's vocabulary while missing entirely the way he looks at things. "The letter" of my article is irrelevant; "the spirit" could be and probably was displayed by Nadel.

More on the Conduct of the Interview

It may be necessary to teach the interviewee what one is looking for (see Gross and Mason, particularly, on this point). But one should in so doing always keep the attitude, which they recommend, that this is merely so that the interviewee can later teach you! They used hypothetical examples to clarify the conceptions which had to be understood in order to deal with the issues which they raised. I myself am inclined to cite contrasts (sometimes actual, sometimes invented) in other jurisdictions or organizations, or to report remarks (sometimes real, sometimes invented) about the situation of concern in the interview. I have practiced modifying accounts given in preceding interviews, to make absolutely certain nothing I say could be traced back to an earlier interview; of course, when a given interviewee knows who the other people you saw in his organization were, you must not attribute anything whatsoever to "other people" that the interviewee could possibly attribute to his colleagues.

Richardson, Dohrenwend, and Klein, Chapter 8, "Encouragements, Silences, Guggles, and Interruptions," are particularly helpful in calling attention to some of the ways in which discussion may be carried on without direct questioning. I suppose, in this very connection, that my self-image of myself as an interviewer was, long before I read Richardson, Dohrenwend, and Klein, one of being poised, pencil in hand, looking intently at the interviewee or listening intently if he seemed not to like being stared at, waiting eagerly for whatever he may say next! Sometimes I will simply say "and . . . ?" A raised pencil is particularly helpful in encouraging the interviewee who is afraid he may not be "giving you what you want" or may be becoming too personal. There are a number of useful discussions of how to get questions answered, *whether they are asked or not*. In addition to Gross and Mason; Richardson, Dohrenwend, and Klein, (especially Part III, pp. 127-268); Nadel; Dollard; and Dexter, "Role"; I should mention Riesman's "Asking and Answering" and Payne on *The Art of Asking Questions*.

There are, of course, periods during the interview when points must be spelled out and made explicit; Payne is very helpful here. Does "everybody" mean "everybody on my side" or "everybody who had power." As an example, I was quite puzzled when a departmental officer said of a colleague, "Nobody was sorry when he left," when it seemed clear that a number of people were. But what the officer meant by "nobody" was "no professional in the department" to which both belonged; people in cooperating departments, clients, and administrative staff were not to him, in that context, "somebody." But the competent interviewer does not irritate the interviewee by directly asking for explicitness on too many such points; he gets at them indirectly.

On Protecting the Confidentiality of the Interview

Powdermaker, who apparently did not type well herself, mentions that of course she could not let an Indianola typist type up her reports; it would not have been safe for her informants. Heard refers to setting up rather awkward office techniques to limit the number of people who had access to his interviews. In general, elite interviewees in the United States and Canada expect confidences to be respected (in large measure, I think, because in their experience newspapermen, attorneys, and physicians have been discreet).

But, as I have reported in my "Good Will of Important People," many scholars are not particularly careful about protecting interviews and interview reports. I suspect that it is the exception rather than the rule when any careful effort is made to see to it that clerks and secretaries who process and handle interview reports and tapes are tight-lipped and trustworthy. Yet, if they happen to have outside connections—for instance, to be engaged in or to have relatives or friends who are engaged in politics—they cannot be expected to maintain complete security unless a very careful effort is made. I have known, for instance, of interviewers who, just to save themselves bother, employed as after-hours typists girls who worked for the same organization as some of the interviewees. The potential conflict of loyalties should have been obvious.

The greatest temptation to secretaries and clerks is probably not the conscious betrayal of confidence but the human tendency to talk about something interesting; "I typed an interview today," they can tell their friends, "with Senator So-and-so, and guess what he said!"

The rule for the interviewer, then, is to make sure that all those who handle interviews are, in effect, "cleared" and have a "need to know," and that, if the interviews leave his hands for the project headquarters office, there is great caution exercised there.

Very dangerous is the tendency of some interviewer-teachers to use interviews as class reading. An interviewer was utterly horrified to find that interview reports, regarding which he had promised complete confidence, were being *read* by an entire class of one of his colleagues, and were being made available to these students so they could write term papers quoting them! The colleague in question seemed to think the interviewer should appreciate the admiration the reports had evoked! They were also made available to several visiting graduate students from other universities. To be sure, a questionnaire had been given to the students to try to detect any manifest contact with people who might want to use the information in ways hostile to the interviewees. But, again, people might talk about interesting things, or some people could have seen ways of selling the information to the press, or contacts could have developed during the course of the semester, after the questionnaire was given.

It is true that the danger, in any given case, of an embarrassing security break is slight. But, if it should happen, and a particular interviewee—particularly a prominent interviewee—becomes upset or scandalized, the results could be catastrophic for (a) the interviewer himself (had some of his interviewees in the situation explained above heard about the free-and-easy distribution of these reports to students, "his name would have been mud," he would have lost access, reputation, and friends), (b) the project (it might have to be closed down; at any rate, foundations and government agencies would be reluctant to supply any further funds), and (c) possibly even for the world of social science research in general. On the principle that catastrophic events which are individually improbable but cumulatively likely should be guarded against, interviewers should take pains to see to it that their interviews are carefully guarded.

Basically, I myself would not now be willing to work on a project where I did not know the entire distribution list of interview reports (provided they involved to begin with an assurance of confidence to the interviewee), and I would insist that I, or some equally security-minded person, should be able to cut anyone off that distribution list on suspicion alone! Furthermore, I would insist that I be given the authority to veto the handling of copies after the project is over; I have seen in the basement of a university building, open to whoever chose to pick them up, reports which I happened to know contained interview statements by several businessmen about ways they had in fact broken the law. No matter how careful project directors are while a project is going on, they tend to get careless after it is over.

(There is an even stronger case for security in regard to tape recordings. One of the major arguments against tape recordings from the interviewee's standpoint is that it is harder for him to say "I did not say that; the interviewer misunderstood," in case confidence is breached.)

Of course, I realize I personally can insist on such conditions because I am not dependent for my living upon employment as an interviewer. A young man or woman, eager to make a professional career, cannot be as demanding. But I would hope the warning contained in what I have said may be remembered! I know of one project where field interviewers were so convinced that a project director was reporting to interested outsiders about the activities of interviewees to the interviewees' disadvantage that they finally decided simply not to record any statements which could be reported in such a manner; although I rather suspect their suspicion was in error, the procedure is worth re-flection.

Conversely, were I to be interviewed about anything where I felt it important to protect confidence, I would insist not only on receiving some assurance that the interviewer himself intended to maintain discretion, but to know what control he had of the reports or tapes after the interview was completed.

The Code of Ethics of the American Sociological Association (as of November, 1968) states in part under Rule 5 on Preservation of Confidentiality of Research Data:

> Confidential information provided by a research subject must be treated as such by a sociologist. Even though research information is not a privileged communication under the law, the sociologist must, as far as possible, protect subjects and informants. Any promises made to such persons must be honored. . . .
>
> . . . the provisions of this section apply to all members of research organizations (*i.e. interviewers, coders, clerical staff, etc.*) and it is the responsibility of the chief investigator to see that they are instructed in the necessity and importance of maintaining the confidentiality of the data. [Italics supplied. I would add that it sometimes happens that the chief investigator is not a field interviewer with elite personnel and therefore is not as aware as the field interviewers of the bargain about confidentiality they often must make, so that, if he is not alert on the matter, they must be.] The obligation of the sociologist includes the use and storage of original data to which a subject's name is attached. When requested, the identity of an organization or subject must be adequately disguised in publication.

This code is of course applicable to interviewers in most other fields.

On Safeguarding Interview Reports and Copies

Of course, it is harder to reproduce lost or destroyed reports of interviews than other manuscripts. It is therefore important to keep extra copies safely. It is, perhaps, not very likely that they would all be destroyed if in the same place; but it is desirable to make sure, if possible, that copies are kept in different buildings, so that in event of fire or other disaster they will not be all destroyed. One exemplary case comes to mind: in shipping his effects from one city to another, Harold D. Lasswell let all his interviews over several years go on the same truck; the truck got into an accident and the interviews all burned.[7] The intended write-up was obviously affected.

On Deceiving the Interviewee: Covert Interviewing?

The standard way of approaching this subject is to say that interviewees should never under any circumstances be deceived. I would prefer to say they should never under any circumstances be harmed. Rosenthal, in *Pygmalion in the Classroom,* reports a case where on an experimental basis teachers were deliberately given false information about their students to see how this information would affect teacher-student interaction; in this case, the false information seems to have benefited the students by causing the teachers to treat them in a way which helped their educational development. According to Rosenthal, when the teachers, after the experiment was over, were informed of the deception, they did not protest.

In fact, to some degree, interviewees, even where the interviewer is absolutely eager to be honest, are deceived; they, almost typically, deceive themselves about the purpose and nature of the project, because they interpret it as being what it would be if they were doing it, not as what it is. An interviewer who was genuinely eager to be completely honest with interviewees would have to *explain* at terribly boresome length and teach interviewees so much social science that he would have to give up being an interviewer!

There is no advantage, and frequently considerable disadvantage, in making such elaborate explanations to interviewees. Of course, it is better not to deceive about the overall purpose; if the project is designed to serve some practical end which they might not approve of, there is an argument for warning them, although, so far as I can see, this is one of the unresolved dilemma areas of scientific ethics. In the 1956 campaign, I purported to be undertaking scientific research while actually I was collecting information designed to help check up on the effectiveness of local Stevenson organizers. It did not occur to me, or to my colleague at the time, that there was anything questionable about this; nowadays, I would feel a bit uncomfortable about it, although actually few individuals were likely to be harmed. I think I would nowadays make a point of refraining from getting interviews with people who might actually be downgraded in the political hierarchy, if I found it necessary to use any such cover story, because they would have a right to feel that the reciprocal trust which is the basis of communication in science and society was being violated; had anybody whom we had seen been removed or downgraded as a consequence of our interviews, he would have had a right to feel that he had been conned.

But, conversely, a state-wide study in which I was involved was made of mental retardates and their families, in contrast with control groups of normals; the study was always described as a "family and health study," although it had little to do with family relationships *per se* and still less to do with health. Yet, no one was harmed, and in fact, some people who might have been chagrined at being included in a study of mental retardates, were permitted to avoid such chagrin.

As a matter of fact, if a scholar really starts out without preconceived notions, he can not be sure who will be offended or regard himself as having been deceived. It certainly never occurred to us in connection with the trade study that the following sequence of events would happen: Our first interviewee, really almost an informant, was an associate of Cleary, Friendly, Gottlieb, and Ball, the well-known Washington law firm which had been active in trying to lobby for import liberalization on behalf of several foreign clients. In the course of the study I decided that the theoretically based procedure which the firm used in trying to gain support for its lobbying had been mistaken. In the duplicated version of my dissertation, I explained why this was so, and Ambassador Ball himself (while in private practice, of course) tried to dissuade me from putting this in print—or possibly his intention was to get me to withdraw it altogether. As it turned out, we did not include this in *American Business and Public Policy,* but not because of his intervention. And another interviewee-informant, an old friend, was a strong, ideological supporter of reciprocal trade. He was horrified at reading my article on "Role Relationships," where I explained how I had adopted the vocabulary and point of view of protectionists in talking to them; he felt I had let him down.

Now, both these interviewee-informants had some basis for feeling that we (or at least I) had deceived them; we had come to them as academics, and they simply assumed that we shared their support for reciprocal trade and their belief in *their* techniques of getting additional support for it. Yet, had we made a big issue at the time of interview of the fact that we did not know where we were going, it would have sounded very ungracious and might have turned out to be a quite unnecessary warning—as most such warnings would be. What I am saying is that any scholar who says "I'll see where the data leads me" is sooner or later bound to deceive some interviewees, from their standpoint. (See Becker on the general issues here.)

In other words, an interview is always to some extent covert to both interviewer and interviewee because the interviewer himself does not know where it is leading!

The practical question then becomes: What are the limits to covertness? Dalton argues that the investigator as such is likely in many situations to be misled if he presents himself as scholar. The man called by Dalton "the masquerading researcher" or "the veiled scrutineer" is likely, he thinks, to get a much more honest picture, a much more correct assessment of some situations. The contention sounds convincing; but we have not enough cases of veiled scrutineers to really demonstrate it. And so we lack reports on the difficulties which veiled scrutineers face. One obvious one is that, in many circumstances, they will be suspected of some sort of espionage. If they can proceed, without unmasking, to the publication of their study, then all may be well and good; but if they are caught making detailed notes, for which there is no obvious justification, while the study is still going on, will they not run considerable risks for themselves and for the reputation of social science in general? I suspect that the announced participant-observer status is a wiser and safer one, although it would be valuable to have comparative experiments— one man acting as a participant-observer in a group, another as a veiled scrutineer, to see who seems to get more insight, what the second learns that the first did not. (Ideally, this should then be followed by a reversal between the same two men in another situation.) I also suspect that would-be veiled scrutineers would profit by taking lessons from detectives or professional spies in how to maintain a role and to take notes and records, for these men have much more experience in infiltration than do social scientists.

One of the problems, of course, that veiled scrutineers would perhaps face would be that of creating ill-will because of a feeling that trust has been abused, friendship betrayed. In a sense, Vidich, during his residence in Springdale, seems to have been a veiled scrutineer; at least, some of the hostility directed against him and his book seems to have been stimulated by the feeling that people had not known they were being studied.

Now, of course, there are ethical problems in the present way of doing research which are probably just as great; but because we are accustomed to them, we do not think about them. Says Dalton (p. 275), "I have watched . . . other researchers [who had told top management what they were doing, instead of masquerading as Dalton did] . . . the smiles and delighted manipulation of [them] by guided personnel . . . the frequently trivial areas to which alerted and fearful officers guided the inquiry." In my own participation in the Katona study of the pricing policies of consumer firms under price control, as I look back, it seems to me that we would have learned far more by masquerading as would-be buyers than simply by interviewing.

The conclusion, if any, is that *any* approach to social science interviewing raises ethical problems.

Informants or Interviewees?

Social anthropologists use the term informant to refer to someone who supplies or collects information to the anthropologist on a continuing basis, who enters into a more or less personal relationship with the anthropologist "in order to bring about cognitive learning on the part of the latter" (Paul, pp. 443-44). Powdermaker's autobiography is particularly helpful because it shows her relationship with major informants; Casagrande has collected accounts of a number of key informants on different anthropological field studies. Whyte's work in Cornerville, as he makes very clear, was heavily dependent upon "Doc" and other informants.

Thomas Rhys Williams gives a set of rules for selecting informants (pp. 28-31), including some suggestions for breaking off relationships with an informant "who appears to be causing harm to general feelings of trust built up with other key informants." Unfortunately, in the situations he has in mind the investigator had some superiority in status as regards the informant, or, where this is not clearly true, the informant had a fair amount of leisure. It is hard to imagine persuading an Emir in Northern Nigeria or a leading Wall Street lawyer to "work as a member of your household," which is one of Williams' suggestions (and a perfectly sound one for his own field work in Borneo). Williams also describes some role-relationships with informants (pp. 48-50) including the tendency towards mutual helpfulness and protection that may grow up. For example, some informants in his experience tend to "protect the anthropologist from aspects of local life considered 'bad,' 'evil,' or 'harmful' (e.g., economic exploitation)." Williams interprets such protection as a "compliment to a friend," but, in any case, he says, "to have such protection offered can provide valuable data concerning definitions in local culture." Thirty years ago, when I was first engaging in the study of political behavior, I remember being told by some interviewees "*You* wouldn't want to know about that," very much the same sort of thing; but at that time it never occurred to me that this statement constituted data; I was merely irritated at being shielded from reality by, for example, church officials who did not feel a young man should hear about seamy church politics.

Williams and other anthropologists discuss what is to be done about lending money (p. 49). "Doc" told Whyte: "There's just one thing to watch out for. Don't treat people. Don't be too free with your money" (p. 14). On the other hand, Mintz makes a point of the fact (p. 6) that he and his major informant would support each other indefinitely if the need arose.

Now, there is practically no discussion, to my knowledge, of informants in studies conducted by people who have not been trained in or greatly influenced by anthropology. Yet, in fact, for some reason or other—interest, desire to teach, inability to find any other comprehending listener, propinquity—even among elite groups, other investigators do get informants. Gusfield tells us that, since he happened to headquarter himself in the W.C.T.U. library, the librarian gradually became friendly to him and passed on "the scuttlebutt." I had for several years been friendly with a congressman and, without ever asking him explicitly, made his headquarters my office, took calls there, etc. I made myself, I hope, of some use by handling calls to him during vacations or lunch hours if everybody else was out of the office, supplying general information on occasions, and becoming friendly with a succession of his assistants; I had originally come to know him by working with him in his first campaign. My hunch is that several later students of congressional behavior have relied heavily upon D. B. Hardeman, research assistant to Speaker Sam Rayburn and later administrative assistant to the Democratic whip (Hale Boggs), as an informant. I dimly realized at the time I was making the trade study that I should seek informants among members or staff of the Ways and Means Committee, and even had two possibilities in mind, but I never could quite figure out how to approach the people whose help I wanted! I think one congressman I had in mind might have responded favorably if I had simply asked him.

It is uncommon to mention informants. There is no mention of my informant anywhere in my writings about Congress, partly because I did not want to make him responsible for anything I said, especially because I have gradually found myself taking a view on some matters quite different from his. In Thomas Anton's outstanding study of budget-making procedures in Illinois, he makes a number of acknowledgments; having visited the Illinois Capitol, my guess would be that two of these people were real informants and the others answered questions or supplied data as asked. Yet, no one could tell it from the book. I would not be surprised to find out that in such a book as Harrison's valuable account of authority in the Baptist churches, he in fact relied upon a few informants for many of his leads. But Anton and Harrison are typical—the reader simply has to guess whether they relied upon informants or not.

In some ways, this does not matter—if their findings check out otherwise. But, for some purposes—for instance, for scholars who would like to replicate their work, it might be important to know how they got their perspective, what sort of "stake," if any, their informant or informants had in the issue. I do not believe—but this is a self-serving belief, not worthy of much credence unless it can be independently checked—that my congressional informant in any way, shape, or manner affected my report! Nevertheless, in reading political community studies which emphasize the importance of powerful decision-makers, as compared with those which do not, I wonder whether part of the difference might be in what kind of informants one scholar or another had.

It is difficult to handle this matter of informants in contemporary American or European studies. I am inclined to wonder whether it would not be worth a closed door conference of scholars who have used informants from more or less elite groups in modern settings to see if any common findings or even important issues to consider emerge. It is obvious that, in most cases, a scholar cannot, in fairness to his informant and his project, say "I depended particularly on so-and-so," for then anything he says which irritates anybody will be blamed on so-and-so—yet, in my case, for instance, insofar as I have expressed views on the congress as an institution or on reciprocal trade policy, they differ markedly from my congressional informant's.

There is a third great difficulty in naming specified informants; I am sure that some of the lobbyists or quasi-lobbyists we talked with felt themselves to be very useful informants also; they certainly went out of their way to supply us with a lot of information! It just did not happen to "take" or to "hit on the key places," and, furthermore, my relationships with most of them did not involve the same mixture of friendship, shared political perspectives, confidence, and mutual respect, as with the congressman. Actually, two of these lobbyists were important secondary informants, because they, like the congressman, were capable of considerable detachment. Others supplied pure data, because they believed in their cause so strongly. Yet I could never publish names attached to such statements.

A conference about informants would consider elite informant utility, the danger of getting tagged as an informant's dependents or protégés (I could not have had the same relationship with any one state legislator in most legislatures as I had with my congressional informant: Congressmen are too busy to notice who is connected with whom; but in all the smaller state capitols at least, connections of the sort I had with him would have made others suspect me), the possibility of getting several informants occupying different positions (I would doubt the feasibility of keeping informants among both the Black Panthers and the Oakland, California, police, without a lot of very time-consuming covert dealings; it would be simpler to have independent studies made by different scholars and integrated later; but in the Congress I could and should have had several informants with different vantage points for my study of reciprocal trade), the rewards one can offer informants (I do not know, for instance, whether any state legislator or official has ever been paid outright to help on an academic project involving study of his office; but, considering the low salary scale, it might be perfectly practical, where legal; or I never found it hurt me anywhere to do minor quasi-political chores in my congressman's office, but perhaps there was some risk; there might be ways I have not considered of rewarding an informant with a lectureship or an LL.D., which some researchers could swing; but, of course, the most important thing to consider is what, on an immediate day-to-day basis, do informants get out of the relationship—part, I suppose, of the pleasure Horace Walpole got in writing to Sir Horace Mann, but how does one enhance that?), techniques of recruiting informants (I suspect that there is a minuet of courtship with many elite members rather than a bare request, crudely offered or refused), and ways of reducing the risks that reliance upon informants may lead one to misinterpret or distort the data.

There are a number of other issues worth consideration. Paul says informants should be representative and must not be recognized deviants (pp. 442-44); Sjoberg, on the other hand, has written an entire article around the contention that marginal men, who, by definition, deviate from the social norm, often make the best informants. Who does make the best kind of informant for what purposes?

And are there studies in which we should rely chiefly upon informants rather than interviewees? I would guess that a mistake in one study in which I was engaged was along this line. I was supposed to interview various persons in Greater Boston about some aspects of the way in which they carried over or used the language of their parents. Although, at a later stage of the project, interviews might ultimately have been useful, it would at least have been helpful for me, in getting to understand the issues and possibilities, to spend considerable time with three or four informants of different language backgrounds. I think, also, such intensive consideration of what was involved would have been more useful for the project.

One warning about informants: There is a tendency, particularly by journalists (who interview the governor once a week, etc.) but also by social scientists, to assume that the head of an organization is *ipso facto* a good informant. This is simply not so; the governor's appointments secretary probably knows far more clearly how his office runs and who wants to see him than does the governor; someone far down in the budget bureau probably has a better picture of what the budget means and how it was put together; someone else knows much better than the governor how his campaign was organized; and so on. Of course, there are exceptional governors; I suppose in my lifetime there have been four governors of Massachusetts who *may* have been worth consulting on these matters (especially Governor Sargent). But there have been nine who clearly were not. Now, of course, one could rarely get a governor as an informant, but the same principle applies to small-town mayors, heads of small businesses, etc. There may be some much better informant in a less prominent post. As a matter of fact, a good many senatorial assistants are better informants than their senators.

Interviewing Abroad

Obviously, my major concerns in this book are with interviewing in the United States and Canada; obviously, as the references to anthropological work in particular show, I think there is a great deal to be learned by interviewers from experiences in other societies. But how much of what is said here is applicable and relevant to foreign interviewing?

I had originally intended to review some of the literature on this matter, but Chaplin, as an outgrowth of his 1968 paper at the American Sociological Association, is preparing a book on foreign elite interviewing. Since he has had experience in this field, which I have not, I am sure it will be far superior to anything that I could do. In the meantime, such accounts as those of Crane, Hunt, and Wahlke, and such studies as those of Deutsch, suggest that there are many similarities and some differences. I do not feel competent to comment at all upon interviewing in ex-colonial nations or those not much affected by European cultural values; Weiner's essay and the related articles in the book in which it appears seem to provide excellent starting points.

It is worth looking at the studies of Jacobson and of Best; each of them was able to interview in different years at least one member from every single United Nations delegation in New York City, apparently obtaining satisfactory interviews in most cases. In the nature of the way in which they got their jobs and of their living situation, most of these delegates were affected by metropolitan values; but, equally obviously, a good many of them were from basically non-European-type cultures.

My impression is that persons affected by metropolitan values, to the degree that it is politically safe for them to do so, will be interviewable, just as members of most elite groups in the United States are. For metropolitan values include some awareness of and respect for research in some form. There are cultural differences; but essentially the problem here is one of adaptation on the part of the interviewers, just as anthropologists obviously have to adapt their manner of getting information to the culture of the particular society they are studying. It is a well-known fact that there is a good deal of "colonialism" in social science research as well as in other aspects of university life, which is to say that people who have been trained in social science at United States institutions are likely to try to use the exact techniques studied in class in new situations. In fact, however, the kind of interviewing technique which worked for me with Congress has to be modified even for Massachusetts state legislators.

Lerner's report on "Interviewing Frenchmen" as a good example of creative adaptation. He found that the kind of approaches which we, on parallel M.I.T. projects, were making in the United States did not gain him very ready access. So he worked out an approach which essentially consisted of asking the French intellectuals in question to consult and advise with him and his staff as special expert consultants. This gained him most of the entree he sought but simply meant posing the issues differently. Where similar difficulties are met in other metropolitan areas, creative scholars can no doubt overcome them with similar ingenuity. Of course, analysis of the significance of what is said and its meaning may demand a considerable knowledge of the society and culture in which the interview takes place; it is perfectly possible that Portuguese intellectuals, for instance, see and experience a social relationship when confronting an American academic interviewer totally different from anything the American academic interviewer has encountered in the United States. But this is only to say that in interviewing in any society or social group one profits by adopting an anthropological viewpoint.

NOTES

[1] Ithiel Pool, a colleague on the trade study project, demurred at the time from my recommendations about technique in the "Role" article and said that he thought challenging people was sometimes a better way to interview. As I think back to the situation, I believe that he was thinking more of our reception and dealings with supporters of liberal trade, who automatically assumed we were "friend" just as most opponents of more liberal trade automatically assumed we were "enemy." I was writing chiefly about how to handle those who regarded us as enemies or at least outsiders; I would agree that we could sometimes learn more from those who accepted us as being on their side by raising questions and arguing.

I think, also, it is relevant to point out that he was, then, altogether a milder-mannered person than I was, then, and that when I argued, I might have provoked resentment, whereas he could argue with less exasperating effect upon his interlocutors. And it is probably also relevant to note that he, I suspect, would have found it then more uncomfortable than I did to act out, in a way which might be taken seriously, some sets of views which he did not hold. I find it interesting and sometimes exciting to see what happens, to hear what I find myself saying, when I act as though I held these unfamiliar views, but I do not think he experienced this role variation as a pleasure to the same degree.

So, for all these reasons, his interviewing techniques would necessarily have been different from mine at that time.

2 In my note, "Interviewing Business Leaders," 1959, I point out a number of reasons for believing that Kincaid and Bright were mistaken in assuming that businessmen in general are unwilling to be interviewed; subsequently, in 1960, on the Garceau project, we again found that most of the prominent businessmen we wished to see were willing to see us—but we wanted to see them about something on which they mostly have opinions, business in politics, and that does not seem to them at all a technical subject (which, even though civil defense is regarded as appropriate and desirable, tends to be the case on that matter).

For any supporter of civil defense, let me say that I would add the words "very unfortunately," after the above statements—see Dexter, "Civil Defense."

3 I did not read Glaser and Strauss until after I had for all practical purposes finished writing this book, but it seems to me, if I understand them, that they make this point of view particularly clear.

4 I should add, however, that in 1956 a colleague and I conducted a set of interviews with San Diego political leaders, explaining that we were working for a foundation which we had to keep unnamed but which was interested in financing studies of factionalism in community politics in several cities. Our interviews were extremely successful—so successful, indeed, that, although our real purpose was one of getting practical political information for the Presidential primary (the kind of covert interviewing in which we then engaged *now* seems to me rather questionable—see the section below on covert interviewing)—it has long seemed to us that we ought to rewrite this material for scholarly use! I am not sure, however, that what worked in mobile San Diego would work everywhere; I would hesitate very much to try the same approach with, for example, the Massachusetts General Court (legislature).

[5] No such studies are, to my knowledge, being undertaken; this is purely a hypothetical example.

[6] Although two comments may perhaps be made:

(a) Recognition of one's own biases and the ability to discount for them is of course important for social scientists and reporters. The interviewer ought necessarily to be *quicker* in recognizing and allowing for his biases whereas in some other situations more time is allowable for discounting them. Accordingly, interviewers can profit particularly from the techniques described by Hayakawa and by Stebbing and by Lasswell, (*Democracy*, Chapter IV) for identifying one's own biases.

(b) Courses in methods of research nowadays, simply because of the proliferation of new research techniques, tend to focus on these external techniques. But as Dollard points out (see Chapter VI below) the "informed intelligence" in contact with the data is, in the interview, the primary research instrument, and therefore the most important way to prepare oneself for research is to improve the capacity of that instrument, to acquire internally the virtues of a good reporter and a good social scientist.

[7] Another kind of safeguarding is also important, especially from the standpoint of the young interviewer. Some years after the Katona study was published, I had an idea as to something which was in our interviews; I was told they had all been destroyed (and I had not kept copies myself). Recently, I was planning to write on a topic on which, some dozen years ago, a competent scholar had interviewed; it occurred to me that some of his interviewees are probably dead, and perhaps he would let me look at them. But it seems that when he changed jobs he discarded all the interview reports.

Conversely, I have kept the interviews with congressmen and businessmen which I conducted in 1953-55 for the trade study; and it now appears that, where interviewees are dead, some could be used or published which would have been very sensitive at the time. It is also probable that the sensitivity of other interviews has long since disappeared, even if the interviewee is alive.

CHAPTER III

**WORKING PAPER ON
INTERVIEWING PROCEDURES FOR
A LAW AND PSYCHIATRY PROJECT**

---

*The following paper was prepared in 1959 under contract to
suggest the interviewing precedures to be followed in a study of
the effect of the Durham Rule (a rule adopted in the District of
Columbia, but not in other jurisdictions, modifying long-estab-
lished legal doctrine about "criminal insanity").*

*The reaction to the paper in typewritten form from profession-
al friends and colleagues led me to plan this present book,
particularly since in the intervening ten years, nothing precisely
like it had, to my knowledge, been issued. On the other hand,
the statement was so unsatisfactory to the project director by
whom it was commissioned that he refused to accept it.*

*I have changed little except to add half a dozen explanatory
but not new points; essentially, the report is presented here as
it was submitted in October, 1959.[1] My impression is that the
practical involvement in a specific research issue which I then
had makes the paper more provocative and useful than it would
be if I now tried to "improve" it, and although there is some
repetition of points already made in Chapters I and II, presenting
them in a different context may serve to clarify them.*

"The interview is a general tool which may be employed in a
variety of particular ways."[2] However, as the writers of the
valuable exposition on the role of "The [Research] Interview:
A Tool of Social Science," soon make clear what they really
mean is that interviewing, viewed abstractly, is a *type* of tool,
and that, just as for particular purposes one particular *sort* of
chisel is more useful than another, so for a particular research
purpose or design one particular *sort* of interviewing is better,
more useful than another.

The reverse also applies: what can *not* be done may also be a function of the tools available, and some kinds of interviewing modify or distort or make impractical some research purposes or designs.

The point of introducing these general reflections at this point is that I have found that my conceptions of what kind of interviewing is to be done are a function of my notions as to how to develop and specify the general research design. This exemplifies, presumably, an advantage of advance reflection about interviewing technology—such reflection tends to lead to additional ideas about what one is looking for, hopes to find, is not interested in, would not see how to handle. But since, in the present instance, I have no intensive knowledge of the history of the project or of the situation which led to it, my assumptions about what to look for may be more or less remote from the basic purposes and concerns of its formulators or of those who carry it out.

The present essay may, however, prove worthwhile for two reasons: (1) Some of the points made apply not only to the research design which is latent or manifest in our thinking as of now but also to a number of other research designs[3] which might be developed for the general project. (2) Sometimes, experience seems to show that presentation of proposals of the sort here made tends to have a "stimulating" value in a Hegelian sense: theses suggest antitheses which may lead to syntheses.

One significant point which is only occasionally touched on in research reports is the kind of recording to be employed in interviews. For this reason, it should be stressed that what the interviewer *records and remembers* is quite as important as what he asks. In interviews of the sort which appear essential here, interviewer understanding of the purposes of the project— *and of the likelihood that in such an "exploratory" study the by-product may turn out to be as significant as explicit answers to specified questions*[4]—is essential; and this means that interviewers must have the intellectual flexibility or breadth of vision to perceive the undefined or the unexpected.[5]

The kind of interview here proposed would be essentially an interview where the "main function of the interviewer is to 'focus' attention upon a given experience"[6] and its effects rather than to ask specific questions. The characteristics of this type of interview may be described as follows:

1. Persons interviewed are known to have participated in an uncontrolled but observed social situation.

2. The hypothetically significant elements, patterns, and total structure of this situation have been previously analyzed by the investigator. Through this situational analysis, he has arrived at a set of hypotheses concerning the meaning and effects of determinate aspects of the situation.

The second point may be modified here to suggest that we are talking about a preliminary analysis of the content of the situation only in terms of quite *general, leading* hypotheses about institutions, reference groups, and the like; for some studies, such as the one under discussion, it would necessarily be premature and misleading to formulate quite specific and definite hypotheses. Resuming the summary:

3. On the basis of this analysis, the investigator has fashioned an *interview plan* which contains a general idea of the major areas of inquiry and the hypotheses (in our case perhaps better called the considerations) which locate (or suggest) the pertinence of data to be obtained in (or from) the interview.

4. The interview itself is focused on the *subjective experiences* of persons exposed to the pre-analyzed situation. The array of their reported responses to this situation or type of situation enables the investigator:

   a. to test the validity of hypotheses (or the pertinence of considerations) derived from analysis and social theory; and

   b. to ascertain unanticipated responses to the situation, thus giving rise to fresh hypotheses.

To this we may add,

5. The interview is more successful when the interviewer can obtain clues, not only through the verbal reports of the subjective experiences but through observation of stance in interviewing, and even more through incidental observa-

tions (not actually part of the question-response interview) of subject's behavior which allow further "insight" into experience. For example, in the studies of congressional and business behavior in which several interviewers including the writer were engaged (the so-called trade study) I think it is true that a fair amount of insight was obtained while waiting for interviews, seeing interviewees talk with subordinates, glancing at their desks, and the like. I believe that more of value would have been learned from these seemingly peripheral observations if at some point in the study I had prepared a careful analysis of what to look for of this sort, or if I even had made a point of recording such observations.[7]

The Framework of Observation: Assumptions within which an Interview Guide Might Be Prepared

[In my original memorandum I made a significant error which showed that I had not grasped a vital distinction between survey interviewing and intensive interviewing. I talked about an "interview guide," which would direct interviewers in great detail (and concomitantly I assumed that interviewers could be so directed). I should have told my client that for projects of the sort he desired interviewers could not be directed by an interview *guide* but must rather take part in forming and revising an interview and study *plan.* My own lack of clarity on this point was not a random or idiosyncratic error but rather represented a systematic failure to distinguish between the problems involved in intensive interviewing and interviewing experts on the one hand from the technique of the standardized, survey interview on the other. It took me seven or eight years to realize my confusion on this point; and I strongly suspect that many people still may be handicapped by this same error.]

In preparing any sort of interview guide or design for study, it is safer to suggest asking about the moderately general rather than the particular, unless one is trying to test rather than to discover.

Our interview design should specify that the main purpose of the interview is to find out the way in which the interviewee tackles concrete cases of criminal responsibility and that so far as possible such information should be obtained together with information that can be related to the interviewee's general handling of his professional responsibilities, his conception of his job and civic responsibility, and so forth. The interviewer should be warned therefore against stressing any particular rule or decision, unless and until the interviewee raises it, *until the very end of the interview.* It might, for instance, turn out that some interviewees are genuinely unaware of the nature of the alleged alteration in practice resulting from recent judicial decisions—but if we started out on the tack of criminal responsibility rather than the more general problems of how they conduct their activities, others will guess that the Durham Rule is in question, and they will feel pressed to express views about it.

In fact, I would prefer that some interviewers be obtained who themselves are quite unaware of the Durham or Mc-Naughton Rules, and who are simply (and honestly) told that they are being hired to find out the social processes involved rather than to collect data about technical legal rules.

The interviewer, that is, would be instructed to start with statements or questions which can be interpreted by the interviewee in several different ways; for example, in my interviews with both congressmen and businessmen on reciprocal trade, *at the beginning* I generally started out by saying that we were interested in learning about the relationship between government and business as it came to the interviewee's attention. Usually, this plus some such question (to congressmen) as "Do you hear much from business?" would lead to an answer or to a comment about what was on the congressman's mind or what he had most recently experienced and from this we could gradually work into the more specific matter of reciprocal trade; in fact, I think I made a mistake by not starting out with even more general questions as "Do you find pressures are intense?" "What do you hear the most about from your constituents?" etc., because it turned out we had to do a lot of guessing as to what some of the reports about "low pressure," and the like meant.

There are a number of such ambiguous questions which might occur to interviewers; my difficulty in writing such an essay or "set of instructions" as this is perhaps not characteristic of inter-viewers in general but may very well be true of a number of good interviewers. I literally find myself thinking of many possi-bilities *in* interview situations which do not occur to me when I am only thinking *about* interview situations.[8] For this and other reasons the interviewers should be given a number of different questions which they might ask—or else instructed in several purposes of the interview without being given specific questions. Among many arguments for this procedure is the fact that in an exploratory study, formal, verbal equivalence[9] cannot at all be assumed to mean actual, sociotransactional equivalence and that the perceptions of a person with a certain type of interviewing insight may permit him to modify a question to allow for differences between different interviewees.

Obviously, the interviewer should be instructed to indicate as best as possible what response-producing comment he used; *but he should also be instructed not to allow ease of recording to deceive him into always asking the same que..tion until he has tried out different ways of getting at a point,* nor should he be guided exclusively by the ease with which interviewees answer given formulations; a more difficult phrasing may tap more meaningful issues.

He should also record the interviewee's answers, of course.

How is he to do this?

Many interviewers can train themselves, apparently, to get significant parts of an interview simply by recording it after-wards from memory. However, in the type of interviewing we are here describing, this seems needlessly risky. Most professional men will appreciate an interviewer's need to take notes, and taking notes will give an excuse for looking back and reflecting if an interview takes an unexpected turn. Notes should not be, on the other hand, so extensive or so absorbing that they deflect attention from the interviewee.

My tactic here is to write down the adjectives, the figures of speech, the phrases that betray the way the man looks at a matter (these can all be abbreviated to consonants), to pay intense attention to his manner of speaking so that I can recon-struct what he has said afterwards with fair ease, and also to record names, places, etc., with some care. (Indeed, where a man may be too quick to let you take adequate notes per se and you are afraid to interrupt the flow of conversation you can slow him up a little by getting spellings right, etc., and add a few other words—particularly if your handwriting is hard to read [like mine] or mixed with shorthand.)

For our purposes it is generally more important to record during the interview itself the style of a man's responses than the substance. To give one very simple example: if several judges always refer to courts in general as "they," not as "we," to "them," not to "us"—this may be a significant clue to attitudes. Yet an interviewer could very well get down the substance of answers on many problems without noting this "little" point.

Or if, as was, I think, the case, elderly protectionists with congressional seniority seemed much more patient and concerned to explain things to me (indeed evoked recollection of the kinds of personal interaction which I felt for my beloved great-aunt) it is this attitude, this concern, which may turn out to be one of the factors that differentiates them from less protectionist men; the worries and concerns which their constituents bring to them they actually do take to heart and don't offset by a concern with "the abstract general good." I am not sure that this difference exists and is significant—partly because I didn't have enough cases for subsamples, but partly because I did not record these nuances as I should have and had to rely on memory months later.

The foregoing examples may, in context, serve to illustrate one of the major advantages of preparation and of continuing revision of an interview plan. It is by no means certain that the observations just made would necessarily have occurred in advance to a project director without his having actually experienced them. Interviewers who make copious records and have an eye for telltale clues would probably have recorded them, had an interview plan been so constructed as to call for them.

David Riesman has said to me: "Above all in interviewing attorneys, be sure to take down a lot." My initial reaction was that this was a fairly useless suggestion. But, in the context just suggested, it now seems to me eminently wise; for preliminary, exploratory purposes, the good interviewer is one who "throws everything into the pot" and sees how it turns out. Nevertheless, when I say everything, I don't really mean everything; but the good interviewer is continuously alert, continuously attentive, continuously eager to add to his notes hunches from observation.

The emphasis upon taking down and noting a great deal, and the suggestion that we may prepare an interview plan, demand consideration of an obvious *seeming* cost involved in such approaches. In the nature of the case, since the budget is more or less final (I understand), adopting this emphasis and this approach means that fewer interviews[10] will be conducted. The underlying reason[11] why this cost may be worth it may be summarized as "the little flower in the crannied wall"[12] principle— careful and intensive study of a few interviews will, in the present instance, combined, of course, with analysis of court records, institutional histories, and other related sources of data,[13] probably illuminate the issues and the subjects more than any effort to conduct and record a large number of interviews.

However, for such careful and intensive interviewing, it is obvious that the interviewers will have to be (a) reasonably skilled, and (b) at least after they have carried out enough interviews so that they no longer have the advantage[14] of naivete, they will have to be encouraged to think imaginatively about what is being looked for and how to deal with the issues at hand. That is to say, I am suggesting the employment of interviewers who can and will collaborate in the preparation of an interview plan for themselves, rather than any effort by you, as project director, me, as consultant, or anyone else to prepare an interview schedule. Recruiting imaginative interviewers may create more administrative work in the early stages of the project but in the later part of the enterprise they will actually save time, I think. The difficulty in the early stages arises out of the fact that there is no very easy way to identify the qualities of imagination and awareness which are desired; negatively, I am sure these qualities are unrelated to formal professional training or to experience in other interview projects. The saving in the later stages will—or at any rate can—come from the fact that in later interviews, interviewers of the sort here described can and will see that they are getting a replay, in slightly different terms, of what they have heard before, and thus be able to short-cut and condense interviews and reports on them.[15]

Some General Remarks on Interviewing Experts

What we are doing here, for the most part, is interviewing experts, and as one of the sources on interviewing which I have recently scanned says: "Nobody knows anything about interviewing experts or about interviews by them. The information we have is almost entirely about how to conduct interviews with random samples of some fairly general non-expert population by people who are not themselves experts."

But several general considerations, which I have not [as of 1959] actually seen stated in print as being of general relevance, are worth presenting:

1. Except in rare instances, exploratory interviews[16] with experts should never attempt to fool the expert or to put something over on him. For some reason, perhaps the market-research origin of professional interviewing, there used to be a very widespread feeling by interviewers that the interviewee has something to hide; and you are trying to "trick" him into telling you about it. [Truer in 1959 than 1969.] Frequently, the interviewee does know something of which he is completely unaware or whose significance may not be apparent to him; but you are generally trying to get his aid and assistance in exploring for this unknown, rather than to pierce his defenses against your inquiries.

2. In general, quite contrary to what many discussions of interviewing suggest, leading questions—particularly negative leading questions—are helpful in interviewing experts; most experts are predisposed to argue about professional matters and set people right, and few of them are so malleable as to fall *tout court* for a leading question. Obviously, limits have to be set; the questions should be respectful and in a style and manner which suggests that the interviewer is worth arguing with or correcting. One useful device of course is to say that unnamed people with whom one has talked (probably members of what is a quasi-out-group—psychiatric social workers, members of a

legislative committee, judges) have suggested thus-and-so; do they care to comment on it?

More on the Development of an Interview Plan

In the Bauer-Pool-Dexter project, and in the Grodzins study, on which I have particularly drawn in making suggestions to you, I did to a considerable degree redefine the problem as I went along. This redefinition in the Grodzins project went as follows: When he first hired me, he was much possessed by the idea that the party system serves as the cement of federalism; as a man with experience in Massachusetts politics, I doubted the existence of a "party system"[17] and did not think party served as a cement but rather, on some matters (such as civil defense), as a disruptive factor; but my interviews led me more and more to see national organizations and professional groups as fulfilling the functions Grodzins initially attributed to the party system, so I more and more asked questions to get light on this hypothesis.

But there was never any formal effort to redefine the problem; the redefinition came out of individual interviews and comments upon them. I think in the present study—and probably indeed more often than not—it would be well to expect a period of redefinition and a reassessment of a fairly explicit and formal nature. Such redefinition would involve and be related to the preparation of an interview plan. Initially, you thought I could prepare an interview schedule. Initially, I said I might be able to do so. On reflection I told you I could not do this, but could merely prepare a rationale of interview procedure. This I have done in the present document; but a more thorough rationale might take place with the preparation of a formal interview plan.

On this point, a general comment and warning may be appropriate. There is a general feeling, probably derived from the necessities of anthropological field work, that the library comes before and after but not really during field work. I don't know why this should be so in Washington; I believe that in the preparation of an interview plan we will see the need and use of some library research which would not occur to us at the present time.

This does not mean, of course, that we will scrap one issue and study another—simply that what may appear to be the issue in terms of initial theoretical constructs is most fruitfully reconsidered in the light of both field work (including interviews) *and* reconsideration of the literature, and such reconsideration should continue well through the project.

Were the writer involved in the matter, he would as of now plan to reconsider after a few interviews the work on role relationships and the sociology of occupations, and he would endeavor to find out if any one has brought together material on the nature of nonlegal sanctions in our society; he would attempt to locate ideas on the nature of innovation from the literature on social and institutional change and read studies about the significance of "opinions" to the personality (attempting to fit it into the role-status conception and into our knowledge of the institutional structure of professions). He would reflect whether the work of Hall, Williams, and others on the sociology of the medical profession has pertinence, etc.

The point here implied is that these different bodies of literature might well suggest modifications in interview planning. Modifications might be considerable; and modifications probably would come also from continuing analysis of interviews, just as in the Bauer-Pool-Dexter and Grodzins projects.

Provided a fair degree of caution and common sense is shown in not trying everything, not biting off more than we can chew, such a theoretic approach seems thoroughly desirable because it permits us to see the Durham Rule in particular and the relationship of law and psychiatry in general in perspective. But the point to remember is that feasible modifications at best are only finite—time and money are limiting factors—and the possibilities which may be taken into account are, if not infinite, quite numerous. I do not know now, for instance, whether the role of reference groups in political sanctions (and perhaps in political or quasi-political factionalism) should be regarded as having high priority for this study or not. Left to myself, in an ideal world, I would say "Yes, of course it should." But new ideas may develop as a result of the interviews; or higher priority may be given to other ideas to which I am now attaching less weight.

In addition, a decision as to what kind of emphasis to place in a study of this sort is not only a matter of response to inputs from the observable data. It is also a decision dependent upon values; Myrdal in *The American Dilemma* supplies us with a classic and relevant statement about the role of values in research.

Obviously, there is one thing to be guarded against in this rather flexible sort of approach to field work and interviewing. Walt Rostow in his military policy study left me entirely free to redefine my objectives in interviewing. I took full advantage of this freedom; the result was that as far as I know the interviews were of no use to him in his analysis; and that, certainly, the published result of my work ("Congressmen and the Formulation of Military Policy") was of no use to him. Interviewers must be kept in touch with each other, so that something may be gained from what they do; if there is a shift in orientation, it is desirable that all interviewers shift; but, above all, it is vital that it be always clear what drumbeat individual interviewers are marching to, so that their interview reports may be analyzed accordingly.

Something on the Mechanics and Ethics of Interviewing

Whether in the interview plan or in earlier preliminary instructions and orientation, some suggestions about the mechanics of what they do will be profitable to most interviewers. This is particularly necessary for some interviewers who have worked on other projects; they may have learned habits there irrelevant to this project, and it is often more difficult to unlearn irrelevant habits than to learn relevant ones from a state of innocence. For example, some of the ways in which survey interviewers treat respondents might well offend judges and psychiatrists (Riesman in Lazarsfeld and Thielens provides an illuminating discussion here).

It is important also to stress the issue of confidentiality.[18] One threat to experts in being interviewed is that the remarks they make may be used against them in a damaging fashion; whereas the modern opinion poll or market-research study *in an urban society* rarely offers any comparable threat to the respondent.

Now we come to a point where I am not in full possession of the pertinent facts, and consequently do not know what can be said to interviewers. Evidently, the interviewer must have some sort of introduction, a copy of a letter previously sent to potential interviewees. He must be prepared for questioning in this, and be instructed if the interviewer does not read it in his presence to explain the gist of it inoffensively. "Now, as background for our study of . . . we would be grateful if you would. . . ," the words following "our study of" being a capsulized description of some part of the project.

But I do not know whether it is essential to call the study one of "law and psychiatry" or have the sponsoring agencies mentioned. With attorneys, such phrases would seem to me very likely indeed to lead to an unfortunate narrowing of the frame of reference and set of recollections. For the conceptions indicated by these phrases and names are by no means neutral—they are almost sure to be taken by a certain number of interviewees as indicating a favorable attitude towards psychiatric technology in the law. This point became very clear to me because in the study of reciprocal trade the mere fact that we, the interviewers, were from a university environment and were scholars meant to some businessmen that we were in the enemy camp, that of liberal trade, and in some instances, to some State Department employees, etc., that we were naturally friends. I would anticipate a much more serious case of the same difficulty here; however, it is only fair to say that I am speaking more in terms of the Boston bar than of the Washington bar, which I don't know; I doubt whether the difficulties due to such phrases would be as great in Cumberland or Frederick, Maryland, where I do know some attorneys, as in Boston.

In any case the interviewers must learn to handle the inevitable questions about the project, about whoever signs the letter of introduction, and about the interviewer himself. Many, although not all interviewees will ask these questions; in some cases they are designed simply to make conversation, but in others they are really means of finding out "are you the type of guy I can trust?" Not having tried out any interviews in the field on your project, I have no idea what assurances can be most readily conveyed to attorneys, psychiatrists, judges, etc. Impressions received from early interviews will doubtless suggest some clarification of instructions on these points.

The interviewers should prepare themselves through study of medical and legal directories, Who's Who, and similar sources, about the interviewee and should also keep their eyes and ears very alert for relevant biographical information in a man's office, etc. Plaques and photographs often help a good deal. Very frequently, background information or a plaque provides a basis for introductory questions: "Do you think your experience in so-and-so affects the way you look at the possibilities of a psychiatric defense when a defendant asks you for counsel?" An advantage of questions of this nature is that they can be asked spontaneously, obviously not from a schedule, and start the interview off as a conversation, rather than as a questionnaire. And of course later on in the interview such pieces of information can be introduced; one can ask a man who seems to have had a good deal to do with wills, or probate, questions about "unsound mind" rather better (and rather differently) than where one has to fish for information as to whether this field of practice is familiar. Or if a man has handled military court cases, this may suggest how to ask questions. And, in fact, ordering of questions may be materially altered by what seems a natural, conversational introduction without any great loss. If one knows for instance that an interviewee has just been engaged prominently in several cases where "insanity" has been an issue, there is no harm in starting off with this topic, although in general the interviewer should *not* clue the respondent to what is desired.

The order of an interview—and the introductory remarks—within broad limits may be best left up to the discretion and feeling of the interviewer about what is natural. The interviewers should, however, be familiar with the dangers involved in introducing specific topics too soon.

One other point which needs to be stressed; there is the proverbial story of the centipede who lay dying in a ditch, because he couldn't figure out which leg went after which, but who, relying on natural reason, had been able to get about satisfactorily. It is often easier to do something, in other words, than to describe or discuss how to do it; my initial reaction to this assignment was, in part, I am afraid, "Well, that's the way I'd interview these people; that's not hard." But, as is by now, I trust, apparent, I was taking a lot of things for granted and assuming that a particular way of interviewing which has usually worked fairly well for me is *the* way of doing things. In the present state of social science, this generalization of one's own experience, although highly necessary in, say, political-campaign research where time is of the essence, is not always safe for work which is designed to contribute to the development of perceptions. In other words, my initial reaction to this problem was a reaction which would be entirely appropriate if I were being asked to help get answers for a practical problem for a practical purpose (for example being asked to aid an attorney in getting information which would convince a jury of something); but I later realized that I was looking at the problem within inadequate limits. That is, I assume that the present project is designed to contribute not only to knowledge of a particular rule and its effects but to enable us to understand the framework within which that rule and its effects should be viewed and to enable us later on to undertake better, more decisive studies in the same field.

Having made whatever preliminary statements are appropriate, the interviewer will then proceed to ask the interviewee (if an attorney) what kinds of consideration he thinks generally go through his mind when considering defense of a criminal. If this needs elucidation, the interviewer will proceed by saying: (perhaps explaining, where he can appropriately do so, his own ignorance) "Would you say that you generally think first of who will prosecute the case? or of the facts of the case? or of the points of law involved? or . . .?" We may fumble a little at the best way of phrasing such questions without suggesting a particular line of answering: The interviewer's *style* in asking such questions, I would guess—that is, impressions about his intelligence and trustworthiness—will matter as much as his precise words. What we are looking for here is reference groups, reference individuals and reference institutions. Who does the attorney think of?

It will in fact turn out that answers to such questions will of necessity determine the order of subsequent questions; but the interviewer will of course need to know what ultimately must be "covered."

With some men, not all, a good follow-up question might be: "Is this the way you would like to do it? Do you think it's best *in moral terms* to think first of (whatever they think first of) or is this simply a necessity of the practical situation?" If there's hesitation, the interviewer can always say "I ask this because somebody whom I recently interviewed said he thought your description of the way attorneys think fits his experience, but he thinks it ought not to."

Having got a picture of whom and what the interviewee thinks of, the interviewer is then in a position to ask about "insanity defenses." For example: "Do you generally consider this as a possible defense?" (if it hasn't been mentioned) or perhaps better, if it hasn't been mentioned, the negative form: "you don't very often think of an insanity defense, I judge?" and then asking why. (One judge of a higher court, who long had a lucrative criminal practice, has answered this question, in my hearing: "All these sons of bitches deserve all and more than all that comes to them; they'd all rape their mothers if they could.") In view of the sponsorship, I would be inclined to use the negative even where an insanity defense is mentioned "but you don't actually find that very useful, do you?" That is, I want to discourage respondents saying what they think we want to hear.

In any case, I would then proceed to ask who the attorney thinks of when he goes to handle an insanity defense—the prosecutor, the psychiatrist or psychiatric organizations, the client or his family—and I would ask such questions as: "Supposing the client or his family insist on an insanity defense when you don't think it's tenable, would you, if you could, bow out of the case or not?"

Since most Washington attorneys have roots or contacts elsewhere, it seems to me fair enough to mention this general fact and add "I suppose you are somewhat familiar with the situation in other jurisdictions? If you were practicing in some other state, would you be more (less) apt to use the insanity defense?" Then, of course, I would ask why?

Then perhaps "If you became a judge in the District, would you be inclined to try to make any changes in the current practice or rulings about insanity defenses? or attempt to alter the way they are handled? What? Why?"

The interview instructions at some point should list a number of issues which the interviewee (attorney) might be expected to have mentioned in response to these and other open questions of the same sort, but specific questions should only be asked on these points after a number of open questions have failed to produce an answer.

Another open question would be perhaps: "Supposing some neighbor of yours or a distant relative, whom you don't know very well but to whom you felt some obligation, were to come to you, not at all as an attorney but as a friend, asking whether an insanity defense should be offered? What would you advise?"

And then: "How about a member of your immediate family?"

Among the points not indicated in the foregoing discussion on which clarification would be desired would be:

1. The respondent's conception of insanity—how does he himself regard it?
2. The respondent's conception of his functions as an attorney —what sort of job or profession does he regard it as? (Questions about what is taught in law school, its real value, or [very apologetically phrased, I would guess, with a plea that the project directors make it necessary?] the respondent's notions about the relationship of law and justice might get at the point.)
3. The respondent's conception of crime.

After having gone over these general points, it may be that the interviewer will feel a certain lack of concreteness—or it may be that several interviews will create a sense of empty generalities. If so, a quite different approach might be tried in which the interviewer asks the respondent to think of specific cases (or hypothetical cases which are described to him) and see what he takes into account. Some interviewers might prefer this method of approach anyway. I have a hunch that my own preference for the general question susceptible of several different interpretations is a function of the kind of person I am—and therefore best, usually, for me in interviewing as a starter, but not per se better than the specific approach (preferred by my colleague, Dr. Davis Bobrow, for instance).

The reason I tend to prefer these general questions, rather than the specific case approach, is that I feel the institutional situation, men's definition of their roles and feelings about them, is best got at by them, and I suppose we are more interested in the institution and the process than in the specific case. But this is a hunch. Practically, I fear specific cases in the man's own experience might involve us in the issue of confidence to the client, and hypothetical cases would take too long to describe— although quite a good interview approach might be worked out by giving a partial description of a hypothetical case and seeing what questions the interviewee asks about it—his questions then becoming "answers" to us.

Obviously, full interview specifications might include a number of other *possible* points to look for, and a number of points to record about the way the interviewee looks, handles the subject, appears to handle other matters, etc. But above all, of course, the emphasis will be on noting style, manner, attitude, references, and imagery—assuming that the orientation I have towards the project is generally acceptable.

So much for attorneys, for the moment. How about psychiatrists? I am not as happy about any general introduction that I have thought of for them—but assuming that psychiatrists are generally reflective and intelligent men, I'd be willing to gamble on an approach which says clearly: "Here we are, both scholars, trying to find something out." In that case, the connection with the sponsoring agent might be stressed rather than minimized; Riesman suggests (in Lazarsfeld and Thielens) that when the status of the interviewer is regarded by the interviewee as potentially or actually inferior to his own, he may address himself to the sponsor of a project, not to the interviewer—for example, college professors interviewed for the Lazarsfeld study on academic freedom were talking past the interviewers to Lazarsfeld. Maybe our psychiatrists will address our sponsors.

This would mean an introductory statement saying:

> We are really interested in all the different ways in which you are (or are regarded by others) as an agent of society.

Some of these happen to come into court; I suppose a lot do not. For example, most of the psychiatrists we have talked with say that the decision to discharge is partly a judicial function. Now, what we are really interested in is: how do you tackle this problem of sanctions? What do you take into account, if anything, aside from what you yourself think of the patient? Do you have any problem reconciling the "social" claim with his "individual" claims? I can ask you a lot of specific questions if you'd like; but maybe you'd just prefer to think about the general problem and start off with your own comments on it

There are a lot of points of course which might be covered by such a question, if it got psychiatrists talking. If it did not, then specific questions could be asked.

An alternative, which would be a little more comfortable to me personally, as of this moment, would be: "Young psychiatrists must sometimes need advice or counsel on the whole series of problems involved in criminal insanity, etc. Looking back on your own career, do you think you received adequate, correct, and useful instruction on these matters?" (If so, what? It not, why not? etc.)

Since psychiatrists who have practiced in one jurisdiction may well have had experience in another, they may be asked to compare different jurisdictions.

They might then be asked to evaluate the way different attorneys, judges, juries, understand and practice insanity defenses. Also they might be asked how far they find it useful to consult nurses, ward attendants, etc., about patients to get some idea of how the layman will react to insanity claims?

Also, suppose they were to be hired by a lawyer as an expert? What do they need to know? What would the main problems be?

Several of the above questions would of course be apt to get at the same points and would not all have to be asked.

Another point—getting at reference groups—"Do you think there is any danger of young psychiatrists taking lawyers as their models, thinking like attorneys, if they do much criminal work?"

These questions presumably suggest a list of points which the interview should cover and which should be outlined in instructions. Interviewing psychiatrists, I would place considerable emphasis upon learning their attitudes towards discharge, where this is either clearly a punishment or clearly a reward.

I would ask them as many as possible of the same questions as I asked attorneys so comparison would be possible—for example, would they recommend an insanity defense to a distant relative, close relative, use it themselves, etc.?

The interviewees should be instructed that the "social rhetoric" of the psychiatrist is of essential importance, and, to get at this in discussing discharges, penalties, rewards, psychiatrists should be asked to specify individual cases by way of example. I suppose that one more familiar than I am now with what psychiatrists do on a day-to-day basis could readily construct a description of circumstances where they do impose penalties or give rewards, including the reward of "being exempt from the normal claim of normality by definition as ill." In discussing such cases, a rather subtle ear for such phrases as "sick" versus "not motivated," "behavior disorder" versus "caught in forces . . ." "won't work in therapy" versus "hopeful prognosis" is necessary—I suspect that the punitive vocabulary of psychiatrists differs far more from that of the average professional man than do his punitive attitudes and it is these latter (as related to role, status, and behavior) which are of the most significant interest.

Another way of getting at the set of problems indicated in the preceding paragraph may be by asking the psychiatrists about "border-line cases" . . . are they criminals or not?

Obviously, those with relevant experience should be asked about cases sent to them for observation, and it might turn out to be important to ask them about the very serious issues posed by court expectations that they "betray" client's confidence. (I suspect that in the actual experience of the average psychiatrist this latter situation, subjectively at least, creates more problems than that of criminal responsibility; supposing a psychiatrist were called to give testimony in a child-custody case about a patient he has been treating?) "Firmness" and the "need for firmness" or "control" is another set of words to look out for when talking with psychiatrists. Anyway, were I undertaking such interviewing, I would regard it as one of my major needs to learn this social rhetoric and its nuances.[19]

For I suspect that the nuances of such rhetoric in fact indicate different roles and role conflicts for psychiatrists within our area of concern.

Until we have thought through such rhetoric and its meaning, our interviews for psychiatrists will have to follow a fairly loose interview pattern.

I have omitted from my discussion hitherto the matters of fact—what sorts of cases, what sorts of practice, how many seen, etc. Some of these can be learned beforehand, many of them will crop up during an interview which is focused as I have suggested, but others will undoubtedly have to be asked separately. The interviewer probably should have a separate sheet with the indispensable factual points which can only be learned from the interviewee. Towards the close of the interview, he should check off what he has learned, and either switch to these, or, if they can be reduced to very brief compass, wait until the interviewee signifies the interview is terminated or the interviewer himself wants to leave to ask them.

I have omitted many points which might have been included and probably ought to be candidates for an interview plan. For instance, should we ask psychiatrists or attorneys in some detail about the allegation that a testator is of unsound mind or that someone needs a conservator because of unsound mind? Does the conception of insanity or the like seem to differ there from what it does in criminal cases?

Were I personally to direct the project, and were the study to cover several different areas which have been discussed, I think I would start with a modest plan for interviewing members of Judiciary Committees (preferably a few in Maryland and perhaps Virginia or Pennsylvania as well as Congress). The reason for this is the practical one that I have interviewed several hundred legislators and would have a framework on which to build; and, all members of judiciary committees are attorneys, and some of them have had a criminal practice. Then I would proceed to judges, who are often ex-legislators and frequently ex-politicians. This is using Powdermaker's technique of starting with easier interviews and learning from them.

Before finally making up an interview plan for the study of psychiatrists I would want to see if I can beg, borrow, or steal an interview plan or sample interviews of pertinence from any of the recent studies of psychiatrists (for example, I do not know if Irving Rosow in his interviews of British psychiatrists recorded his interviews or prepared an interview guide); I estimate altogether there are [as of 1959] about 40 studies which could possibly be pertinent. Ditto with studies of the legal profession. I suspect the time to study such data if available would be after the exploratory interviews. Many seemingly relevant efforts could on the basis of experience with exploratory interviews be scanned and dismissed; but if scrutinized in advance of any field work would consume time from the project director.

It is worth commenting upon two reasons why (aside from personal factors) the project director may have rejected my report entirely. In the first place, he had in mind the notion that I, as a technical "expert" on interviewing, independent of the project, could prepare an interview schedule. He assumed that one would naturally standardize the approach to different respondents. Although I told him explicitly and repeatedly in the conversation when he hired me that I would prepare a "rationale," he still expected an interview schedule. My guess is that, with the increasing use of standardized interviewing since then, even more project directors would now have such expectations. My point is partly that an effort to standardize actually may destroy rather than increase comparability and meaning; interviewer X can raise questions in one way with Y, but if he uses the same technique with Z the meaning is altered. But if the interviewer is sufficiently sensitive he or she can ask Z questions which do get at the same cluster of meanings as have been elicited from Y by the other technique.

More generally, I was assuming—but did not formulate in a way which made it clear to the project director—that is, it was self-evident to me but I did not really say it very clearly—that interviewing can not be considered independently of the problem and the situation. Interviewing is a matter of strategy and tactics, as Phillips explains.

Glaser and Strauss, in showing us how a grounded theory can best depend upon comparability of categories and properties, may perhaps help avoid misconceptions of the type that I believe I did not overcome here. Had their analysis been available to me I might have been able to convince the project director that, in a study of how criminal law is carried out, we need to vary questions and observations in the fashion they suggest, rather than to rely upon Procrustean interview schedules.

NOTES

[1] Most of the footnotes, however, are either added to take account of more recent developments or further knowledge on my part and are thoroughly revised. Some trivial footnotes in the original have been deleted. Footnotes 3, 4, 5, 10, 11, 12, and 14 are given as in the original.

[2] The quotation is from Maccoby and Maccoby.

[3] This "Working Paper on the Law and Psychiatry Project" of course is *not* in itself a research design; but research designs in a fruitful project may be compared to onions; the first skin is but a beginning and there are a large number of other skins to follow. The first several discussions normally only define parameters (and those tentatively) within which designs may be developed.

[4] The classic example of a by-product becoming central to a study was the finding of the Hawthorne experiment wherein it appeared that the sense of being valued was the most important variable in stimulating production, rather than the technical side (see Roethlisberger and Dickson).

[5] In discussion with the project director in June, 1959, I suggested several interviewers, skilled, experienced, in the normal sense abundantly qualified. But on the basis of the analysis in the text above it becomes apparent that some of them are not really qualified for this particular project although they did excellently in other projects. In other words, not only must the interview vary with the research design, so also must the interviewer. (The point is that these interviewers were good survey interviewers but not good specialized interviewers or elite interviewers—the one skill does not guarantee the other. And some persons who would be good specialized interviewers with old-style rural politicians or with business executives might not do so well with forensic psychiatrists —or vice versa.)

[6] I am relying here upon Merton, Fiske, and Kendall, and upon Jahoda *et al.*, 1st ed., I, 176-77. However, it is worth noting that

the general underlying approach to theory here was (unconsciously) much closer to Glaser and Strauss than to Merton. My am-
bivalence about an "interview guide" shows that I was going away
from Merton without being aware of what I was doing.

[7] Preparing an interview guide would have been a desirable idea
if the interview guide had been more than an interview guide. That
is to say, what is really needed is a statement which helps observers
try to think about what kind of data they want to observe, record,
remember, and elicit.

Like a good many other things—for instance the use of tape
recorders—which in and of themselves are good ideas, it may more
often than not be too time-consuming to prepare a formal statement
about what to observe, etc. But where early interviews and observations do not seem to lead anywhere—where one does not seem
to be getting organizable data for the purposes—such a statement
will, I think, be helpful. That is, it should be regarded as something very likely (but not necessarily) to be prepared after some
exploratory interviews have been conducted, if at that stage there
is dissatisfaction or ambiguity.

Subjectively, for the investigators this may be desirable too; if
exploratory interviews do not seem to be getting anywhere, the
preparation of such a statement or guide appears far more practical
and active than just worrying about what is somehow not jelling.

My guess is that on this project some such effort might at some
time have been worthwhile for the particular project director—not
because it was per se necessary but because the early interviews
would have been unsatisfactory to him, because, *I guess,* he really
did not know if he wanted practical findings about how better to
apply the Durham Rule *or* theoretic observations about the sociology
of law and the politics of psychiatry. *Preparation of a manual or
statement on what kind of data to collect might have forced him to
establish priorities.*

If I continue with the comparative study in state government
mentioned elsewhere in this book, I suspect I ought to prepare a
statement about what kind of data to elicit, observe, collect, and
record. Maybe then I will discover what I am really looking for,
or why my project needs redefinition. As of now, I am as unsure
as the director of the law and psychiatry project was then.

[8] A parallel: I am told that a number of contestants on quiz shows
actually think of answers under pressure which "they didn't know
they knew"; and to a limited extent, when I thought I was going
to be a contestant on a national quiz show and was preparing
myself by intensive viewing, I found myself coming up with many
answers (quicker than the contestants) that I'm sure I couldn't

otherwise have given, "otherwise" meaning in a normal nondemanding situation.

[9] Throughout this discussion, as is developed in Chapter VI below, the notion of "transactional" is that worked out by Dewey and Bentley in *The Knowing And The Known.* See also Bentley, *An Inquiry Into Inquiries,* and the last chapter of Bauer, Pool, and Dexter.

[10] One possible way in which, in this particular study (and other studies of this type), on-going analysis might have paid off, even in budgetary terms, may be mentioned. The preparation of preliminary analyses of the sort here indicated (for the interview plan as suggested would have been a preliminary analysis) would probably have made it easier to get additional funding than would otherwise have been the case—assuming the interview guide were to be done well, of course.

[11] It should be noted, in fairness to the project director, that this paragraph in the text and the following one contain ideas which may not have been clear to him; although they were intended by me, my original formulation probably was too elliptic; these two paragraphs are completely revised from the original text.

[12] The reference is to Tennyson's "Flower in the Crannied Wall," 1870.

> Flower in the crannied wall,
> I pluck you out of the crannies . . .
> Little flower—but if I could understand
> What you are, root and all, and all in all,
> I should know what God and Man is.

Less metaphorically, a number of distinguished biological and social scientists have pointed out that detailed analysis of one case may be more instructive for some purposes than an effort to study a number of cases.

[13] In this text, as I wrote it, I assumed such use of nonreactive materials (that is materials not obtained from interviewing or conversation, or from stimuli created for purposes of the study). I did not emphasize this assumption enough; and until very recently indeed I would have regarded such materials as merely "supporting." Indeed, I still find myself writing "supporting" as the modifier of materials. I am reasonably certain that the project director, as a matter of course, because it was the "up-to-date" social science technique assumed he would rely upon interviews; and I am quite sure that I—with the professional bias of the man who is accustomed to, and has done well in employing, a given technique—never stopped to wonder how much we should rely on interviews.

[14] Some interviewers can benefit from not knowing very much about a subject; however, in a study of this sort, the interviewees would necessarily, after a while, teach them a good deal about it; they could not preserve the benefits of ignorance for long.

[15] To some extent, I took advantage of this kind of familiarity with what interviewees were likely to say both in the Bauer-Pool-Dexter trade studies and in the Grodzins study. I skipped over things which were obvious from the early interviews and raised new questions in the later ones about issues I had not previously thought of and/or went into more depth and detail in the later ones on issues superficially covered in the earlier ones. Probably this gradual change of orientation should have been recorded; in fact, I was never aware of it until the preparation of this essay forced me to think through what was in large part of intuitive response to experience on my part.

[16] One advantage of the emphasis upon a few exploratory interviews at the beginning in preference to starting out to do a large number of interviews may be mentioned; in regard to any sensitive subject (and I assume that this one is) there is always the fear that one may upset a given interviewee a good deal. Since the set of respondents in this study will, many of them, know each other, a very negative reaction from any given interviewee may have harmful results in getting cooperation from others. Now, simply cutting down the number of initial interviews (and so far as possible confining them to people who may be expected not to be unusually prickly or negativistic—for instance not interviewing to begin with those judges believed to be unusually sensitive about the sanctity of the bench) reduces the likelihood of such unfortunate reactions. Then, too, if they are told that the interview is exploratory and tentative, they probably will be less inclined to make trouble as a result of a misunderstanding or a mistake, and more inclined simply to tender advice.

So far, this footnote is a revision of a footnote accompanying the original report; as I look back on it now, I think I should also have suggested that throughout the project all interviewees be told—judges and psychiatrists are, after all, more sensitive about professional confidence than people in most professions (or at least this is a general impression)—that the whole project was an exploratory and tentative one to see if judges and psychiatrists should and could be profitably interviewed. This approach would, I think, have tapped the advice-and-counsel-giving tendency many people in these professions have and would have reduced still further the risk of any unfortunate reaction. Subsequently, to be sure, Grey, Becker, and (see especially) Glick have all successfully interviewed judges; it is interesting that, between 1959 and 1965, several social scientists to whom I mentioned this paper expressed blank surprise at the idea that judges could be interviewed!

[17] A definitely discursive example of why I felt this way: In 1949 John F. Kennedy, then a young congressman, was asked to be a major speaker, along with the two leading Massachusetts Democrats at the time, Secretary Tobin and Governor Dever, at a banquet. He demurred, having various other preferred engagements, and when pressed, said "Why should I do it?" One of the delegation which was asking him said "Congressman—for the sake of the party!" He paused and then replied "The party—the party—the party! Just what in the hell is the party? We've done pretty well, hitherto, in Massachusetts on the principle of each man for himself and the devil take the hindmost, and I, for one, don't propose to change it!"

[18] In the original text, I pointed out one issue of confidentiality which the interviewers and project directors would have to take into account, especially when interviewing judges about the application of a new rule. Did interviewers—and the project staff—have any full protection from being forced to testify (or more practically getting into trouble for refusing to testify) before a congressional committee? The courts might, no doubt, *ultimately* be convinced that there was an issue of separation of powers here; this would not protect the interviewers or project staff from harassment and embarrassment if a congressional investigating committee became interested.

Aside from that, I was not and am not certain what would be the case if there were reason to suspect that the interviewers or project staff had acquired information which would suggest there had been illegal or illegitimate procedure in a given case. There is not, to my knowledge, any protection afforded interviewers, similar to the seal of the confessional.

There is another issue of confidentiality which had never occurred to me in 1959, but which became much more realistic during the Kennedy administration. It is best illustrated by my interviews with congressmen, newspapermen, and defense department officials on military policy for Walt Rostow. Professor Rostow promised, and presumably kept, a complete security guard on these interviews as sent to him in 1956-57. But when Walt Whitman Rostow became a chief military advisor to the president, could his memory keep such a security guard? If he noted or remembered something relevant to his obligations to the president in these interviews which might help in relations with a congressman (even though embarrassing to the congressman?), did he forget it? *Did he even necessarily remember where he learned it?* I do not know that there was any such item anywhere in my interviews, because I have only a vague idea of the Kennedy-Johnson administration's handling of military matters in relation to the Congress; but there could have been!

Now, in fact, the kind of people who might have been the very best interviewers for the Durham Rule project for which this report was written might well have been the wives of young attorneys, who, later on, might have become judges, or taken cases regarding the interpretation of the Durham Rule—or they might have been wives (or patients!) of psychiatrists involved in its interpretation. And the project directors were the kind of people who might very likely have become appellate judges in the District of Columbia; supposing the interviewers had got relevant, specific, personal information from lower court judges of a sort not ordinarily known to higher courts—could and should former project directors have forgotten such information?

[19] Pool, 1939, unfortunately still unpublished is still the best empirical treatment I know of social rhetoric; see also Kenneth Burke.

CHAPTER IV

ON ORAL HISTORY INTERVIEWING
by Charles Morrissey

Although this informal statement is explicitly directed toward oral history interviewing, it in fact is an excellent description of how any sort of elite interviewing should be undertaken. The remarks were made by Mr. Morrissey to the First Colloquium on Oral History (Elizabeth I. Dixon and James V. Mink, eds., Oral History at Arrowhead, pp. 68-77, copyright by the Oral History Association, reprinted here by permission). There have been a few deletions and minor changes.

Mr. Morrissey explains his connection with the Kennedy and Truman oral history projects in his commentary. He is now Director of the Vermont Historical Society at Montpelier, Vermont. He has published a number of articles on oral history, and is editor of The Oral History Newsletter.

Perhaps this will strike you as an unorganized presentation on oral history interviewing, but I think perhaps it's the only way in which to do it. Let me make a few prefatory observations about techniques. My experience has been restricted almost entirely to political figures—those who have been elected to public office, or those appointed to public office. The more I've discussed oral history with various people, the more I've become impressed with the fact that techniques and other aspects of oral history vary with the type of person you're interviewing. My experience with political figures might be different from someone who is interviewing people in medical research, scientists, early alumni of the University of California, or people in other professions. Likewise, with any large category of people there are individual variations. I interviewed fat old tired congressmen and bright young men who came to Washington with John F. Kennedy, in some cases younger than I. It is an unusual experience to be interviewing someone on Kennedy who is not yet thirty-one years old.

A lot depends on the interviewer, and I'm talking now about a single interviewer. We have tried team interviewing, but I'm rather lukewarm about it. In some cases it's worked out well, but it all depends on the person you're talking to. To some people, three is a crowd; others enjoy having several people around the table. For the most part, however, we prefer one interviewer facing one interviewee. We think that works out best.

A lot depends on the interviewer's background: how much prior research he's done; how many interviews he's already conducted; that is, how many interviews he's conducted on the subject that he's going to discuss with the person before him today. Did he have a preliminary, exploratory interview in which to discuss the project and the procedures? That very definitely has an influence on how he would conduct the interview.

How much control does he have over the situation confronting him? Once, I went to interview a senator [Jacob Javits], and was told I could have only twenty minutes with him. Then I was kept waiting forty minutes before getting in to his office, so obviously this is a factor. When you're rushing for an airplane, if you've done four interviews and you have a fifth one coming up, you're not in the best of shape to really focus on the fifth one. (I've done as many as five in a single day, in a city away from home.) You're tired, your're run-down, you're confused, and in some cases you can't remember if the person you're interviewing said something to you five minutes ago, or if somebody you interviewed earlier in the day said something to you; that very definitely affects your technique. A lot depends on how much control you have over your situations.

Let me say that to reduce interviewing to a set of techniques is, as one person put it, like reducing courtship to a formula. Gould Colman has pointed this out; Elizabeth Dixon has pointed this out in some of the things she's written about the UCLA project. There is a danger of too much reliance on tools and not relying sufficiently on old-fashioned intuition as to which tool to use in which situation.

It's very easy to be critical of how someone does an interview. You've probably heard the story of the football player who ran back the opening kickoff of a game for a touchdown. The coach called him off the field and criticized him for not doing things right. He cut the wrong way; he used the wrong arm to straight-arm somebody, and so forth; and the player said, "How was it for distance, Coach?"

We should truly play it by ear, so what follows is meant to be taken in a cautious, tentative way. It will sound much more didactic than it is intended. Nevertheless, I want to distill my experience with interviewing about 90 people on the Kennedy project and about 15 on the Truman project.

We had what we called volunteer interviewers at the outset of the Kennedy project, about 135 of them, who did a total of about 300 interviews. When I say volunteers, I mean journalists, people in the administration, colleagues of people to be interviewed, friends, all sorts of arrangements, put on a kind of person-to-person, informal basis. There were two other interviewers working with me full time on the Kennedy project, and it was my responsibility to train them and supervise their work.

In dealing with both President Truman and President Kennedy, our interest was episodic. We'd interview a person on his association with each of these presidents. We were not strictly autobiographical in getting his whole story. This obviously has problems; when you interview someone like Averell Harriman, you'd like to get the whole story. But our purpose was to focus on the Kennedy chapter or the Truman chapter and hope that, someday, somebody will get the rest. We just couldn't do everything.

One of the things we emphasized was to let the interviewee talk. It's his show. Let him run with the ball. As Louis Starr said, "A good interviewer is a good listener." Oftentimes we would start by saying, "When did you first meet John Kennedy?" or "When did you come into his orbit?" He would take off, usually chronologically; this might turn into a topical treatment, just running on haphazardly; I would sit and listen. There's a value to this because he's volunteering what's foremost in his recollections.

While this was going on, I would often sit with a notepad and pencil, just writing one or two words about things he had covered, or things I wanted to come back to. Before the interview started, I would tell him that I would take notes, in the sense of trying to get down just a word here or a word there, or perhaps asking him later for the correct spelling of a name he mentioned. We always carried a notepad with us when we went on an interview.

After he had run through his story, I would often go back and interlace my questions with what he had already said, trying to probe deeply into certain matters, raising points he missed, asking for examples of generalizations he had given.

In phrasing our questions, we found it most important to leave them open-ended, that is, not to indicate in the phrasing of the question the answer you expected to get. We would not offer alternatives and say, "Was it this way or that?" or "Was it either this way or that way?" We would try to state the question in such a way as to get him to pick his own alternative, because he might come up with one that we had not anticipated. We would avoid the loaded word. On the film of the interview done at Berkeley, that word "lobbyist" bothered me. Some people aren't "lobbyists": they are "public relations consultants," "industrial representatives," or something else. We would try very desperately not to impress our own conclusions on the answers the man was giving. It is very hard to restrain yourself, but one way we would try to do it would be to phrase our question, "To what extent was such and such so?" not, "Was such and such so?" We would not try to build a case like a lawyer trying to build a case in a courtroom. I used to advise people to read the Warren Report, because so many times the attorney would say, "This is the way it was, wasn't it?" and the witness would say, "Yes" or "No." And right down the page, the answers are yes or no. We went at it saying, "Tell us how it was; describe it in your own words," to let the interviewee volunteer what he thought was important.

I advise people to read the transcripts of Lawrence Spivak's program, "Meet the Press," and then do it just opposite from the way he does it. Those transcripts are available, incidentally. It is worthwhile to see how someone can phrase a tricky question in trying to trip up someone being interviewed on that program.

We would of course avoid jargon, and for academic people that's difficult. Many people in Washington don't like academic people and don't understand academic publications because of the jargon. Dean Acheson, among others, has spoken very forcefully on this point.

We would try to focus in our interviews on the dynamics of how policy was developed, the actual development of policies. This may seem obvious to us, but many of these volunteer interviewers we had on our project would ask a man in 1964 or '65 how he appraised policy developed back in '61 and '62. We wanted to know how that policy developed, and then, perhaps, conclude with his appraisal of it. One guideline I would stress, perhaps above all others, is that a good interviewer should pursue *in detail*, constantly asking for examples, constantly asking people to illustrate points they are making.

A good interviewer should not allow intimations to pass into the record without elaboration: specifically what did the person mean by such and such? We would try to keep our questions brief and pointed. At most, a question, in our opinion, should occupy no more than two sentences: one sentence to say, "This is why I'm going to ask you this question," and then, "This is the question I'm asking you," ending the question with a question mark, and then sitting, biting the lip, keeping quiet, letting the man think (hopefully), letting him answer the question. It's difficult to endure, that embarrassing silence that bothers so many of us socially when we talk.

In oral history one of the great dangers is for the interviewer to feel that he has to keep talking until the interviewee tries to get a word in edgewise. I think, sometimes, the interviewer tends to rush things. We should let the interviewee set his own pace; if it is slow, from our viewpoint, nonetheless it is his pace. We should let him go at his own rate. With the volunteer interviewers in the Kennedy project, we found, time after time, that they were rushing the man from one point to another, and we actually had cases of the man saying, "Just a minute, can I say something about that last point, before you rush on?"

People often ask about mike fright. Are people afraid of the mike and the tape-recording equipment? Our experience with the Kennedy volunteer interviewers was that *they* were more scared of the equipment than were the people being interviewed. Most of the people being interviewed were familiar with microphones; they had spoken publicly; they had dictated their own letters into dictaphones; and so forth. However, many of the volunteer interviewers were new to operating tape-recording equipment and were uneasy with it. They didn't know whether they were doing the right thing, whether the volume was high enough, whether the mike was close enough, and this sort of thing. It bothered and affected the quality of the interview.

When there were very tough questions to be asked, we learned to postpone the tough ones until the interview was well under way. Obviously, we wanted to establish good rapport; the longer the interview lasted, more times than not, the man would relax, open up, and even enjoy the occasion. Likewise, if we asked tough questions, the man might take offense, and that would affect the remainder of the interview. The definition of a tough question varies for different people. Some people were offended when we raised the question of John Kennedy's religion as a factor in the 1960 election, which strikes us as a very normal question for a political scientist or historian to ask about. Also, if we had several tough questions to ask, we would never ask them consecutively. We would ask one, handle it, and then try to move the interview into an area we wanted the man to talk about, so he would relax and enjoy it; then perhaps later, we would come back to another tough one.

In phrasing the tough ones, we often did what book reviewers do: "Some readers might object to the author's tendency to do such and such," which really means, "I object to his tendency to do such and such." We'd say, "Some people have reported that you got into difficulty on such and such a project." In other words, we're asking him to answer these anonymous people who aren't in the room.

Constantly in our interviews, if we had an important subject we wanted to cover, we would return to it from different angles. Let's say we were interested in the West Virginia primary of

1960; so we'd ask about it, why Kennedy defeated Humphrey. Later, if we were talking about how the Kennedy campaign was organized, we might move back into West Virginia from a different angle, such as the Kennedy organization in West Virginia and how it was set up. If later we were talking about public-opinion polls, we'd move into the West Virginia primary from that angle; if we were talking about campaign finances, we'd move in from there; and if we were talking about the relationship between John Kennedy and Hubert Humphrey throughout their political careers, we'd move in from there. We were always amazed at how a different approach on a different topic would produce new information. The danger, in other words, is to think a matter has been entirely discussed when you cover it once, drop it, and then don't come back.

In the course of all this, we would try to find out how good the man's memory was. We would throw in little questions, sometimes, to test it. For example, if he mentioned the name of a person named Lawrence, we'd say "Is that the Lawrence that was governor of Pennsylvania or the Lawrence who writes for *U.S. News and World Report?*" And we would say, "Did that happen before or after something else happened?" And these little clues someday, we assume, will help the researcher who's reading the transcript or listening to the tapes to decide how much weight he should put on the testimony of this person.

Likewise, we would try to find out, indirectly, how close the person was to the events he was discussing, if he was intimately involved or on the periphery. We tried to ask questions to bring this out. And many times somebody would admit, "Well, no, I wasn't there when that happened, but I heard about it afterwards." And that of course has great bearing on how much weight a historian should put on it.

We tried to find out who was involved in a certain matter—let's suppose, how the Peace Corps speech was prepared in the 1960 campaign. Who was where? Who worked on what draft? and so forth. This obviously has leads for the future; and in interviewing other people, you can ask them about it.

We would also ask a lot of these people what other evidence would exist for the things they were talking about. Would there

have been a memorandum on the subject? Or did some news-
paperman with entree have something reliable in his column on
that particular subject? Did he keep a diary? Was there exchange of correspondence on it? And, as a result, in the long
run the oral-history transcripts at the Kennedy Library will say
an awful lot about the documentation in conventional written
sources pertaining to the Kennedy Administration.

We would try not to miss the obvious, even if it seemed silly
to cover the obvious. For example, somebody would say, "I was
responsible for getting voters registered in the Mexican precincts
of Los Angeles." Well, to him, I suppose, this was an obvious
task, but we wanted to know exactly how you go about it.
Where do you start? What do you do? And we'd ask him to
elaborate on some of these procedures that people in public
office and public affairs conduct.

We'd often use documents in our interviews; that is, if the
man's memory was poor, let's say on the 1948 campaign, I'd have
an itinerary of where Truman spoke in that campaign, each stop,
right through the day. Or we'd present a picture of the people
who were present at a certain occasion. By seeing the people who
were there, he might say, "Oh yes, this fellow helped us with
the draft of such-and-such." Or we'd show him newspaper
columns and say, "How does this represent your impressions of
how such-and-such happened?"

On other occasions, we'd set up a hypothetical adversary. This
is a technique that Forrest Pogue of the George Marshall Library
has used. He'd say to someone, "You were present when Roosevelt
died, and someday someone is going to write a book saying
Roosevelt was murdered. How would you answer that?" And of
course the fellow would offer all sorts of evidence in response
to it.

There were many times when we were stuck. We were covering matters we didn't know much about, so we'd rely on the
old-fashioned journalistic technique of who, what, when, where,
how, why, and so forth.

Also, constantly in the course of interviewing we would try
to put ourselves in the position of the person being interviewed.
We'd try to visualize the web he operated in, if he had worked

with people in Congress, in the White House, in the Bureau of the Budget, and in other departments, the press, lobbyists, or the Democratic National Committee. We would try to visualize how he must have operated with all these other people in Washington, and in that way try to think of questions that would perhaps bring to light some of these relationships.

We'd also try to put ourselves in the place of other students who would be interested in what this person had to say, and suddenly the oral historian becomes an economist or sociologist, or he says, "If I were a biographer of John Kennedy, what could this person offer about the biography of Kennedy? If I'm a student of public administration, what can he offer about certain procedures that were conducted?"

We'd ask ourselves, "How does this fellow spend his day? Where does his time go?" And if you could figure that out, you could figure out what questions to put to him.

We sent our transcripts back to be edited by the person interviewed. In the eyes of many people, this is considered to be an indulgence to the interviewee. We used it as a second opportunity to ask questions we didn't think to ask in the first interview. We would ask for the elaboration. We'd clip a question to the side of the page and say, "Senator, could you give an example of this?" In some cases, if a man had not covered a subject in the transcript, we would leave a blank section. "Would you mind writing in ink some more on this?" With that blank paper in front of him when he went through the transcript, sometimes he would actually sit there and fill it up with two hundred and fifty words or so, and contribute some material that was valuable.

Also, if you chicken out in an interview and don't ask the tough questions, you can always ask them when you send the transcript back to be edited. I think the key question in assessing an oral-history transcript is really not how much material does it provide for history, but rather, how well did the interviewer do with the circumstances affecting him and the material he had to work with? You can't blame the interviewer if the interviewee has a bad memory. But you can blame the interviewer if he doesn't take advantage of every opportunity available to him. And it seems to me that's the key question. If the interviewer did the best he could with what he had, you can't blame him for the results. If he did less than that, you can blame him, and I think he should be blamed appropriately.

Let me say that very little has been written about techniques of oral history. I hope in the future that we can have workshops on this to bring to bear our varying experiences to help the un-initiated, perhaps to see actual transcripts and have the inter-viewer explain why he did certain things and didn't do others. Likewise, I think somebody very productively could prepare a thirty-minute tape with three voices on it: an interviewer, an interviewee, and a narrator, the narrator saying why the inter-viewer is doing this, or if the interviewer makes a mistake, the narrator perhaps pointing out what the mistake is and what he could have done that is different.

Interviewing, in conclusion, is very difficult when you think that the good interviewer must know his stuff; he must be listen-ing to what the man is saying; he must think of more questions to ask; he must be thinking of what the question was he just asked, to make sure the man is answering it. He must know what's already been covered; know what he has yet to cover. He must anticipate where he's going to go if the man, while he's talking, indicates he's about through with the subject; and in anticipating where the conversation is going to go, he must in his mind be beginning to try to formulate the next question so it will come out well-phrased. It's a very difficult business. Any-one who does it successfully is probably so successful that he should himself be interviewed.

CHAPTER V

**WHAT KIND OF TRUTH
DO YOU GET?**

"How Do You Know If the Informant Is Telling the Truth?" by John P. Dean and William Foote Whyte

Research workers who deal with interview data frequently are asked the question: "How do you know if the informant is telling the truth?" If they are experienced research workers, they frequently push aside the question as one asked only by those unsophisticated in the ways of research. But the persistence with which it comes up suggests that we take it seriously and try to formulate it in respectable terms.

Those who ask the question seem bothered by the insight that people sometimes say things for public consumption that they would not say in private. And sometimes they behave in ways that seem to contradict or cast serious doubt on what they profess in open conversation. So the problem arises: Can you tell what a person *really* believes on the basis of a few questions put to him in an interview? Is this not a legitimate question?

The answer is, "No"—not as stated. It assumes that there is invariably some basic underlying attitude or opinion that a person is firmly committed to, i.e., his *real* belief. And it implies that if we can just develop shrewd enough interviewing techniques, we can make him "spill the beans" and reveal what this basic attitude really is.

To begin with, we must constantly bear in mind that the statements an informant makes to an interviewer can vary from purely *subjective* statements ("I feel terribly depressed after

The late Dr. Dean was Associate Professor of Sociology and Anthropology at Cornell University, Ithaca, New York; Dr. Whyte is Professor of Industrial and Labor Relations at Cornell University, Ithaca, New York.

the accident") to almost completely *objective* statements ("The Buick swerved across the road into the other lane and hit the Ford head on"). Many statements, of course, fall somewhere in between: "The driver of the Ford was driving badly because he had been drinking"; or "It was the Ford driver's fault because he was drunk."

In evaluating informants' statements we do try to distinguish the subjective and objective components. But no matter how objective an informant seems to be, the research point of view is: *The informant's statement represents merely the perception of the informant, filtered and modified by his cognitive and emotional reactions and reported through his personal verbal usages.* Thus we acknowledge initially that we are getting merely the informant's picture of the world as he sees it. And we are getting it only as he is willing to pass it on to us in *this particular interview situation.* Under other circumstances, [what] he reveals to us may be much different.

Granted this, there are two questions that the research worker wants answered: (a) What light does the statement throw on the subjective sentiments of the informant? and (b) How much does the informant's report correspond in fact to "objective reality"?

I   THE INFORMANT'S REPORT OF "SUBJECTIVE DATA"

The problem here is how to evaluate the informant's subjective report of what he feels or thinks about some subject under investigation. At the outset we must recognize that there are different kinds of subjective data that we may want the informant to report: (a) A *current emotional state* of the informant, such as anger, fear, anxiety or depression. Many informants have great difficulty in putting feelings of this sort into words. Even for the most articulate, the verbal expression of complex emotional states is a difficult thing; (b) *The informant's opinions,* that is the cognitive formulation of his ideas on a subject; (c) *The informant's attitudes,* that is, his emotional reactions to the subjects under discussion; (d) *The informant's values,* that is, the organizing principles that underlie his opinions, attitudes, and behavior; (e) *The informant's hypothetical reactions,* that is, his projection of what he would do, think, or feel *if* certain circumstances prevailed; and (f) *The actual tendencies of the informant to behave or feel* when confronted with certain stimulus situations. Generally, of course, verbal reports are only part of the data on the basis of which we infer persons' tendencies to act. Equally important in making these inferences are past behavior and a variety of non-verbal cues that we may detect.

Each of these various kinds of subjective data are elicited by different kinds of questions put in different ways to the informant. The assumption that any one of these represents his "real" feelings in the matter is, of course, unwarranted. For one thing, the informant may have conflicting opinions, values, attitudes, or tendencies to act. In fact, the conflict among these various subjective data may be the most important subjective information we obtain. This approach puts in quite a different light the problem of using behavior as a way of validating attitudes. Take, for example, a young housewife who in an interview expresses herself as much in favor of careful budgeting of household finances. She indicates that she and her husband have carefully worked out how much they feel they can afford to spend on various categories and have even gone so far as to make out envelopes in which they put the money allocated to these various purposes. Subsequent to the interview, however, she goes shopping with one of her close friends with whom she feels a good deal of social competition. Under the pressures of this situation she buys a dress which is out of line with her financial plan. It is not very meaningful to say that her behavior in buying the dress "invalidates" her opinions in favor of budgeting. Nor does it make sense to ask what her "real" attitudes toward budgeting are. But because we often expect reasonable behavior in the management of personal affairs and daily activities, we frequently try to get informants to give a rational and consistent picture of their sentiments and behavior when confronted with them in an interview situation. If this young housewife had been asked by the interviewer what she would do if she ran across an unusually attractive dress which was not within her budgetary planning, she might have said that she would refuse to buy it and would incorporate some budgeting plan for the future by which she might be able to purchase such a dress. But the sophisticated researcher does not expect informants to have consistent well-thought-out attitudes and values on the subjects he is inquiring about.

The difficulties in interpreting informants' reports of subjective data are seriously increased when the informant is reporting not his present feelings or attitudes but those he recollects from the past. This is because of the widespread tendency we all have to modify a recollection of past feelings in a selective way that fits them more comfortably into our current point of view.

But perhaps the major consideration that makes the evaluation of reports of subjective data difficult is the fact that they are so *highly situational.* If, for example, a Democrat is among some Republican friends whose opinions he values highly, he will hesitate to express sentiments that might antagonize or disconcert these friends. If, however, he is among his own intimate friends who think pretty much as he does, he will not hesitate to express a Democratic point of view and, if he is at a Democratic party meeting where there is considerable enthusiasm in support of party causes and he is swept up in this enthusiasm, he may express Democratic sentiments even more strongly than among his own friends. *The interview situation must be seen as just* ONE *of many situations in which an informant may reveal subjective data in different ways.*

The key question is this: *What factors can we expect to influence this informant's reporting of this situation under these interview circumstances?* The following factors are likely to be important:

1. Are there any ulterior *motives* which the informant has that might modify his reporting of the situation? While making a study among the foremen of a South American company, the researcher was approached one day by a foreman who expressed great interest in being interviewed. In the conversation which followed, he expressed himself with enthusiasm about every aspect of the company under discussion. When the interview closed, he said, "I hope you will give me a good recommendation to the management." His ulterior motives undoubtedly influenced his reporting.

2. Are there any *bars to spontaneity* which might inhibit free expression by the informant? For example, where an informant feels that the affairs of his organization or his own personal life should be put forward in a good light for public consumption, he will hesitate to bring up spontaneously the more negative aspects of the situation.

3. Does the informant have *desires to please* the interviewer so that his opinions will be well thought of? An interviewer known to be identified with better race relations might well find informants expressing opinions more favorable to minority groups than they would express among their own friends.

4. Are there any *idiosyncratic factors* that may cause the informant to express only one facet of his reactions to a subject. For example, in a follow-up interview, an informant said that she had changed her attitude toward Jews. She then recalled that just before the initial interview a dealer had sent her a wrong couch and she implied that he had tried to cheat her. She recalled that he was Jewish and that she was still mad about this incident and reacted in terms of it to the questions about Jews in the interview. A few days earlier or a few days later she would probably have expressed herself quite differently. Idiosyncratic factors such as mood, wording of the question, individual peculiarities in the connotations of specific words, and extraneous factors such as the baby crying, the telephone ringing, etc., all may influence the way an informant articulates his reactions.

Unless they are taken into account, these various factors that influence the interview situation may cause serious problems and misinterpretation of the informant's statements. To minimize the problems of interpretation, the interview situation should be carefully structured and the interview itself should be carefully handled in the light of these influences. Outside influences should be avoided by arranging an appropriate time and place for interviewing that will eliminate them as much as possible.

The influence of ulterior motives can sometimes be quashed by pointing out that the researcher is in no position to influence the situation in any way. Bars to spontaneity can usually be reduced by assurances to the informant that his remarks are confidential and will be reported to no one else. The confidence that develops in a relationship over a period of time is perhaps the best guarantee of spontaneity, and informants who are important should be developed *over time* with care and understanding. Naturally the interviewer should not express, or indicate in any way, his disapproval of statements made by the informant or indicate any of his own values that might intrude in the situation. Idiosyncratic factors of connotation and meaning are difficult to account for, but it is certainly a good precaution to ask questions in many different ways so that the complex configuration that a person's sentiments represents can be more accurately understood.

While we never assume a one-to-one relationship between sentiments and overt behavior, the researcher is constantly relating the sentiments expressed to the behavior he observes—or would expect to observe—in the situation under discussion.

In one field situation, the informant was a restaurant supervisor. It was already known that the restaurant owner was a graduate dietician who placed a great deal of stress upon maintaining high professional standards. Midway in the course of the interview, the supervisor remarked in a casual manner—perhaps too casual—that she herself was the only supervisor in the restaurant who was not a college graduate. The supervisor did not elaborate on the point, nor did the interviewer probe at this time. In a lull in the conversation a few minutes later, the interviewer, using the opportunity to return to a topic previously mentioned, said: "I was interested in something you said earlier: that you are the only supervisor here who is not a college graduate—." Before another word was uttered, the supervisor burst into tears. Clearly, the affect attached to the statement made earlier was repressed or concealed and became evident only as revealed in subsequent behavior when she cried.

In some cases the informant may be trying to tell himself— as well as the interviewer—that he does not have a certain sentiment, and may even have convinced himself. In the case of Joe Sloan, a gasoline plant operator (see the article on "Engineers and Workers," *Human Organization*, volume 14, no. 4, winter, 1956), the interview took place shortly after Sloan, a highly ambitious worker, had been demoted to a lower classification. He followed up this rebuff by talking with the plant manager and personnel manager, and he reported calmly that they had not been able to give him any encouragement about his future with the company. Since, even before this setback, Sloan had expressed strong negative sentiments toward management—with apparent relish—one might have expected him to be even more explosive, now that he had this new provocation. The researcher was surprised and puzzled when he said, "I'm nonchalant now. Those things don't bother me anymore." Neither his gestures nor facial expression revealed any emotion.

A week later, Sloan suddenly walked off the job in response to a condition that had recurred often in the past, with only mild expressions of dissatisfaction from Sloan and the other workers. Reflecting on the incident later, we can see that we should have recognized Sloan's "nonchalant" statement as a danger signal. In the light of the recent events that must have intensified his negative sentiments toward management, he must have been making an effort to repress these sentiments. Probably, being unable or unwilling to "blow his top" as before, he no longer had a safety valve and might have been expected to take some rash and erratic action.

These cases suggest the importance of regarding any marked discrepancies between expressed sentiments and observed (or expected) behavior as an open invitation to the researcher to focus his interviewing *and* observation in this problem area.

II THE INFORMANT'S REPORTING OF "OBJECTIVE" DATA

Frequently the research worker wants to determine from an interview what actually happened on some occasion pertinent to the research. Can we take what the informant reports at face value? In many instances the answer, of course, is "No."

Suppose an informant reports that a number of people are plotting against him. He may be revealing merely his own paranoid tendencies, in which case his statement must be seen as casting light primarily on his distorted perception of the world. But even though plots of this kind are rare in the world, it may just happen that, in this instance, people actually *are* trying to undermine the informant. It is therefore important for the researcher to know in what respects an informant's statement must be taken as a reflection of his own personality and perception and in which respects as a reasonably accurate record of actual events.

How much help any given report of an informant will be in reconstructing "objective reality" depends on how much distortion has been introduced into the report and how much we can correct for this distortion. The major sources of distortion in first-hand reports of informants are these:

1. The respondent just did not observe the details of what happened or cannot recollect what he *did* observe, and reports instead what he supposed happened. Data below the informant's observation or memory threshold cannot of course be reported.

2. The respondent reports as accurately as he can, but because his mental set has selectively perceived the situation, the data reported give a distorted impression of what occurred.

3. The informant unconsciously modifies his report of a situation because of his emotional needs to shape the situation to fit his own perspective. Awareness of the "true" facts might be so uncomfortable that the informant wants to protect himself against this awareness.

4. The informant quite consciously modifies the facts as he perceives them in order to convey a distorted impression of what occurred.

Naturally, trained research workers are alert to detect distortion wherever it occurs. How can they do this? First of all, there is an important negative check: *implausibility*. If an account strongly strains our credulity and just does not seem at all plausible, then we are justified in suspecting distortion. For example, an informant, who lived a few miles away from the campus of a coeducational college, reported that one of the college girls had been raped in a classroom during hours of instruction by some of the men college students. She was quite vague as to the precise circumstances—for example, as to what the professor was doing at the time. (Did he, perhaps, rap the blackboard and say, "May I have your attention, please?") This account was obviously lacking in plausibility. Things just do not happen that way. The account may, however, throw light on the informant's personal world. Through other reports we learned that a college girl had indeed been raped, but the offense had taken place at night, the girl was not on the college campus, and the men were not college students. The woman who told this story was a devout member of a fundamentalist sect that was highly suspicious of the "Godless university." In this context, the story makes sense as a distortion the informant might unconsciously introduce in order to make the story conform to her perception of the university. The test of implausibility must be used with caution, of course, because sometimes the implausible *does* happen.

A second aid in detecting distortion is any knowledge we have of the *unreliability of the informant* as an accurate reporter. In the courtroom, the story of a witness is seriously undermined by any evidence that he has been inaccurate in reporting some important point. In first interviews we will generally have little evidence for judging an informant's reliability unless he happens to be reporting on some situation about which we have prior knowledge. But in repeated interviews, after what the informant has told us has been checked or corroborated by other reports, we can form some idea of how much we can rely on his account. Thus we learn to distinguish reliable from unreliable informants, although we must always be careful not to assume that, just because an informant has proven reliable in the past, we can continue to believe his accounts without further checking.

A third aid in detecting distortion is our *knowledge of an informant's mental set* and an understanding of how it might influence his perception and interpretation of events. Thus we would be on guard for distortion in a labor union leader's report of how management welched upon a promise it made in a closed meeting.

But the major way in which we detect distortion, and correct for it, is by *comparing an informant's account with the accounts given by other informants.* And here the situation resembles the courtroom setting, since we must weigh and balance the testimony of different witnesses, evaluate the validity of eyewitness data, compare the reliability of witnesses, take circumstantial evidence into account, appraise the motives of key persons, and consider the admissibility of hearsay information. We may have little opportunity in field research for anything that resembles direct cross-examination, but we can certainly *cross-check* the accounts given us by different informants for discrepancies and try to clear these up by asking for further clarification.

Since we generally assure informants that what they say is confidential, we are not free to tell one informant what the other has told us. Even if the informant says, "I don't care who knows it; tell anybody you want to," we find it wise to treat the interview as confidential. A researcher who goes around telling some informants what other informants have told him is likely to stir up anxiety and suspicion. Of course the researcher may be able to tell an informant what he has heard without revealing the source of his information. This may be perfectly appropriate where a story has wide currency so that an informant cannot infer the source of the information. But if an event is not widely known, the mere mention of it may reveal to one informant what another informant has said about the situation. How can the data be cross-checked in these circumstances?

III

An example from a field study of work teams at the Corning Glass Works illustrates this problem. Jack Carter, a gaffer (top man of the glass making team), described a serious argument that had arisen between Al Lucido, the gaffer and his servitor (his #2 man) on another work team. Lucido and his servitor had been known as close friends. Since the relationship of the interpersonal relations on the team to morale and productivity were central to the study, it was important (1) to check this situation for distortion and (2) to develop the details.

First, the account Carter gave of the situation did not in any way seem implausible. Second, on the credibility of the witness, our experience indicated that Jack Carter was a reliable informant. Third, we had no reason to believe that Carter's mental set toward this other work team was so emotionally involved or biased as to give him an especially jaundiced view of the situation. Furthermore, some of the events he described he had actually witnessed and others he had heard about directly from men on the particular work team. Nevertheless, to check the story and to fill in the details regarding the development of the conflict, we wished to get an account from one of the men directly involved. So an appointment was scheduled with Lucido one day after work. Because it might be disturbing to Lucido and to the others if the research worker came right out and said, "I hear you recently had an argument with Sammy, would you tell me about it?" the researcher sought to reach this point in the interview without revealing this purpose. Lucido was encouraged to talk about the nature of his work and about the problems that arose on his job, with the focus gradually moving toward problems of cooperation within the work team. After Lucido had discussed at length the importance of maintaining harmonious relationships within the work team, the research worker said, "Yes, that certainly is important. You know I've been impressed with the harmonious relationships you have on your team. Since you and the servitor have to work closely together, I guess it's important that you and Sammy are such close friends. Still, I suppose that even the closest of friends can have disagreements. Has there ever been a time when there was any friction between you and Sammy?" Lucido remarked that indeed this had happened just recently. When the researcher expressed interest, he went on to give a detailed account of how the friction arose and how the problem between the two men had finally worked out. It was then possible to compare Lucido's account with that of Carter and to amplify the data on a number of points that Carter had not covered. The informant in this case probably never realized that the research worker had any prior knowledge of the argument he had with his servitor or that this matter was of any greater interest to the researcher than other things discussed in the interview. The main point is this: by the thoughtful use of the information revealed in the account of one informant, the researcher can guide other interviews toward data which will reveal any distortions incorporated in the initial account and usually will provide details which give a more complete understanding of what actually happened.

The problems of distortion are heavily compounded if the researcher is dealing with informants who are giving him second-hand reports. Here, the researcher has to deal, not only with the original distortion that the witness incorporated in the story he told to the informant, but also with any subsequent distortions that the informant introduced in passing it along to the researcher. Of course, an informant who has a shrewd understanding of the situations about which he is reporting secondhand may be able to take into account any distortions or bias in the reports he receives from those who talked to him. It *may* even be that the informant's lines of communication are more direct and intimate than the research worker can establish. In this case, the picture the informant gives may have validity beyond the picture the researcher might get directly from the eyewitnesses themselves.

This kind of situation is illustrated by the case of Doc, a street corner gang leader discussed in *Street Corner Society*. Doc was an extraordinarily valuable informant. Whenever the information he gave could be checked, his account seemed highly reliable. But he had an additional strength: he was also well-informed regarding what was happening in his own group and in other groups and organizations in his district. This was due to the position he occupied in the social structure of the community. Since he was the leader of his own group, the leaders of other groups naturally came to him first to tell him what they were doing and to consult him as to what they should do. His informal leadership position within his own group made him a connecting link between that group and other groups and organization. Hence developments in the "foreign relations" of the group were known by him before they reached the followers, and usually in more direct and accurate form.

Because of the wide variation in quality of informants, the researcher is always on the lookout for informants such as Doc who can give a reasonably accurate and perceptive account of events the research is interested in. These special informants are frequently found at key positions in the communication structure, often as formal or informal leaders in the organization. They have ability to weigh and balance the evidence themselves and correct for the distortions that may be incorporated from their sources of information. But it is important that they [should] have no needs to withhold or distort the information they report to the researcher. Even so, wherever the researcher has to rest on second hand reports he must be particularly cautious in his interpretation.

In conclusion, we should emphasize that the interviewer is not looking for *the true attitude or sentiment*. He should recognize that informants can and do hold conflicting sentiments at one time and they hold varying sentiments according to the situations in which they find themselves. As Roethlisberger and Dickson long ago pointed out, the interview itself is a social situation, so the researcher must also consider how this situation may influence the expression of sentiments and the reporting of events.

With such considerations in mind, the researcher will not ask himself, "How do I know if the informant is telling the truth?" Instead, the researcher will ask, "What do the informant's statements reveal about his feelings and perceptions and what inferences can be made from them about the actual environment or events he has experienced?"

The above article is reprinted by permission from Human Organization, *vol. XVII, no. 2, (1958), copyright by The Society for Applied Anthropology. The remainder of the chapter is by Lewis Anthony Dexter.*

Facts, Inference, and Analysis

For the purposes of most social science interviewers, Dean and Whyte have made the central points. Although they focus on *informants*, most of what they say is equally applicable—although perhaps more difficult to apply—in one-shot interviews. The chief practical difficulty in such interviews is the obvious one: the less acquaintance one has with an individual, the harder it is to determine what biases or reasons for deception, ingratiation, etc., may affect what he says.

There are two general issues on which it would be helpful if more could be meaningfully said. In the first place, a good many interviewers are simply concerned with "hard fact"; did such and such an event take place? Detectives and others engaged in criminalistics, oral historians, sometimes journalists, and, most obvious of all, military intelligence interrogators, on many occasions are simply using interviews as substitutes for direct observation, because, for one reason or another, direct observations are hard to undertake. There is great need for a thorough rethinking of the use of the interview as a testimony and evidence of fact; such rethinking would include, but by no means be confined to, the kind of points made by Webb, Campbell, Schwartz, and Sechrest, and the issues raised in the present book. At one time, I reviewed some literature about social science interviewing to see how it might be of aid to the military interrogator concerned with hard fact; although the resulting report is not uninteresting, as I reread it and look at the items in an accompanying bibliography, I believe that there needs to be some fusion of experiences and tests of validity from a whole series of fields before highly satisfactory work of this sort can be achieved; at any rate, to try to deal with this matter here would at least double the size of the present volume.

A second issue which is suggested by Dean and Whyte is that of inference; what kind of inference can be validly drawn from what kinds of interview reports? Again, in order to deal with that problem satisfactorily, we would need to discuss much which is not otherwise germane in this book. But there are several works that are moving in the direction of answering the question, and these will repay careful study; among them I find Cicourel particularly challenging. What is needed, however, is the presentation of specific interview reports with a spelling-out of the inferences drawn from them, sentence by sentence, and a statement of the reasoning justifying the inferences. Here again we come to a crucial consideration for interviewers; it is very important to keep old interviews. By and large, when elite and specialized interviews are new, they can not be published in such detail as to make any analysis of inference and validity possible; it would be a crude betrayal of confidence. But although I could now publish some of the interviews I conducted on, for example, the trade study 15 years ago, I nowhere recorded the inferences I was making. In fact, like most elite interviewers, I think, I did not formulate the chains of inference as such, so that any effort to handle these interviews in that way now would be a reconstruction rather than a presentation of data.

I reflect the attitude of many interviewers, I think, when I point out one additional difficulty in this proposal. When I am absorbed in interviewing, or in reconstructing a pattern on the basis of the interviews, I find myself somewhat annoyed by talk about methodology. Much interviewing and some analysis of interviews seems to me to have some of the characteristics of political speechmaking or even of writing poetry; the frame of mind is not conducive to logical analysis of presuppositions. This attitude was responsible for considerable resentment which I felt at a suggestion that I should add a methodological appendix to my work on the trade study; it seemed to me a bit like asking an imitator of Anthony Trollope to give us a formal, schematic account of the process of representation in his novels.

I am not at all certain that any complete reconciliation of the tension between the observer-discoverer who makes imaginative leaps and has fun playing with patterns, on the one hand, and the analyst on the other is possible. I suspect, however, that an awareness that the tension exists and that it is desirable to shift roles explicitly from discoverer-observer to analyst would help some interviewers to explain why they inferred what they inferred. I presume that here, as elsewhere in the progress of knowledge, art and science are not really antithetical; rather, people who have learned or developed a certain kind of art at a certain stage in their own careers find it bothersome and time-consuming to add other skills or points of view later on. I think, also, that if any one had thought it worth the effort to take particular interviews and ask me why I reached the conclusions I did, what the process of reasoning was, I would have filled in gaps. In other words, left to do it all myself, I did not like the idea of formulating what I was doing, but might have found it exciting if somebody else had *interviewed me* about my interviews. Some support for this statement is found in my reaction when Morton Grodzins actually spent three days cross-questioning me on my Massachusetts and Maryland interviews for him on federal-state relations; I found the experience interesting and rather fun.

RELEVANCE

There are a couple of points in regard to "truth" and inference in the interview which deserve comment at the present time, even though there is not, as far as I know, any worked-out analysis in terms of which they can be handled. "Error" is, as Peter K. Manning points out in one of the significant articles on the interview, not absolute but rather better described as "error in terms of the model of meaning with which I am proceeding and by which coherence is said to obtain in the situation." Granted Dean and Whyte's argument that the interviewee tells some sort of truth about himself when he tells us anything at all—that is he gives us true data about *something* if we but have the wit to interpret it—granted even the correctness of a statement by an obscure eigthteenth-century Swiss proto-sociologist to the effect that "men chatter through their fingertips, even when they are silent with their tongues"—nevertheless, the particular data which is being given us may be irrelevant, so far as we can see, to our model of meaning. The first task, undoubtedly, and one which from quite different standpoints is urged on scholars by writers like Dean and Whyte, Sidney and Beatrice Webb, Dewey and Bentley, and Lasswell (*Psychopathology*), is to see if by re-defining our model of meaning, our sense of what is coherent, we can use the data which we are given and get somewhere. Given the tendency towards the fallacy of misplaced concrete-ness, there is great value in constantly keeping in mind the possibility that the data we are in fact getting will serve to organize relevant theoretic constructs, even if it is not given to us in the terms in which we asked it. It is precisely in order to avoid this tendency that matter-of-fact, institutionally common-sensical writers like Sidney and Beatrice Webb warn us against premature closure by supposing we know all the questions and are just looking for answers; it is interesting to find forty years later the high methodology of Glaser and Strauss emphasizing very much the same approach.

Nevertheless, Manning is quite right in indicating that the data we get from a given set of interviewees may be quite use-less in explaining the particular problem with which we were concerned to start with. I have never clearly had this experience myself with a set of interviewees; but it is perfectly possible that the physicians[1] whom Manning, and before him Oswald Hall, interviewed, by taking a position of "evasiveness or implausibility, free to ignore the demands of the questioner who is stepping out of his deference role," (Manning, p. 307) were thereby failing to provide Manning or Hall with any data which could be used to organize the patterns or explain the issues with which the latter were concerned. (I should add that I have had a number of *individual* interviews which were clearly failures in precisely these terms: for example, on the price-control study, a meat-packer insisted on simply calling the OPA names, but when I asked for specifics he reacted by indignantly saying "Are you calling me a liar?") There is, I think, at present no way of being *certain* that a given set of interviews have failed, provided a fair amount has been said; for it is possible that future analysts might make sense out of a collection of statements which at the moment do not seem relevant. I have certainly had the experience over the years as I have mulled over my congressional and trade-study interviews of seeing a good deal in them which I did not initially recognize—although it took me fourteen years to become aware of some of the relevant implications.[2] But we can reasonably assume that some sets of interviews are failures, and have not communicated truths relevant to our concerns, even though we can not be sure of this.

A much more systematic and coherent way of determining when interviews are in fact failures might be worked out by developing a theory of explanation (taking, probably, as a starting point the work of Robert Brown) which can be applied to an interview or a set of interviews: under what circumstances do interviews as analyzed provide data and inferences which lead to some sort of explanation? Since Brown's own training and field work was in anthropology, one would wish he might carry forward efforts of this sort! Such a theory of explanation for the interview would, I suspect, have to go back to F. C. S. Schiller's sadly neglected doctrine of relevance.

In the meantime, we can suggest three kinds of circumstances where interviewees are particularly likely to give irrelevant answers:

1. When there is a more-or-less professional *contempt* for the interviewer—(I am distinguishing contempt here from hostility; hostility may, if it is thought the interviewer will understand, produce useful comments, but contempt is less likely to do so). "For example," says Manning in a letter to me of March 12, 1968,

> one female physician whom I interviewed told me afterwards that I ought to look at her bookshelf to see all the useful AMA publications and . . . to understand the many "positive func-tions" which the AMA performs. . . . I told her that I was well aware of these and was, in fact, impressed with them as well. She responded that she felt she had to point this out to me since all my questions were loaded. . . . My questions were not loaded, I think they were fair. The point is, that they identified me with a position, by virtue of my being a sociology student.

It is a reasonable hypothesis that in a good many environments with a good many physicians any sociology student who was not blatantly pro-American Medical Association would be re-garded as being contemptibly anti-AMA by those physicians who cherish membership in it. Analogously, many respectable Boston suburbanites with a "Harvard accent" could not have received straightforward answers in the 1930's to questions about politics from many Boston municipal officials, unless they had gone out of their way to make clear they did not hold the "goo-goo" (good government) views expected of them. As a class, they would have been regarded as incapable of understanding—i.e., intellectually contemptible.

2. Where there is an undue desire to ingratiate oneself with the interviewer or those who sponsor his project. Back and Ger-gen describe the interview as a conversation with a purpose; in this conversation, they say the interviewee may be regarded as playing two games—one involving the satisfaction of expressing his own views, etc., is the information-giving game; the other, that of "establishing rapport" with the interviewer, called by them the ingratiation game (pp. 2-3). To the extent that, for whatever reason, the latter game becomes dominant, it will be-come very much harder—and often impossible—to get relevant data on any subjects except those bearing on the interviewee's

notion of appropriateness, courtesy, friendliness, and ingratiation. In unstructured interviewing, therefore, it may with some interviewees be important to avoid giving unnecessary cues as to the kind of answers desired, or to give offsetting cues, so that the interviewee who is eager to ingratiate himself is forced to feel, in a way, "I don't know what you want."

3. Finally, there is one other situation, which, though it may contain elements of ingratiation, goes well beyond it. Like strains of bacteria that have learned to be resistant to antibiotics, interviewees in certain social groups in the United States have learned to be interviewed. Like Kluckhohn's Navajo informant who said "I don't know; let's see what the published anthropological works, hidden behind the curtain in my hogan, say," they may no longer reply with information from experience, but with the kind of information which, previous interviewers have taught them, is desired. In view of the fact that the whole schooling system tends to teach people to give "the right answers" as seen by teachers and textbooks, it is quite natural that many interviewees in our society should be predisposed to learn the right answers in early interviews (or from classroom study of social science) and then regurgitate them for the benefit of later interviewers. Put another way, a process of adult socialization may be going on, which, incidentally, has the result that certain classes of interviewers are destroying the natural resources upon which their profession depends, much like the lumber barons of the nineteenth century who laid waste great stands of timber. When I was interviewing on Capitol Hill in 1953-54 I was the only full-time social science interviewer there, and I suspect many of my congressional and lobbying interviewees had never been interviewed by a social scientist previously. Nowadays, it must be a very rare specimen who lasts a year on Capitol Hill without being interviewed, and I have been told of at least two congressional offices where it is estimated that the congressman and his top staff spend at least a day a week being interviewed and otherwise informing social science students! I have been told, also, of seven distinct interviewing studies going on in one narrow area of a Negro section of Boston; and in Birmingham, Boston, and other cities, one of the expressed gripes of black leadership is the multiplicity of studies of which they are "victims."

One of the needs of the profession as a whole is to find out what kinds of accommodation, contravention, or objection take place in response to this process of interview and re-interview. Of course, as I point out in "The Goodwill of Important People," the irritation which such repeated requests for interviews create provides a reason for trying to direct researchers and students away from "the hot social problems" and the fashionable research sites of the moment—of course, this contention will be strenuously rejected by some policy-oriented social scientists. In reply, I would argue we can learn more about policy by studying less-studied issues, but this leads to a number of other considerations which there is not space to discuss here.

As a practical matter, I think anyone beginning a project might well take into account the probability that (a) hot and fashionable subjects are being overstudied, (b) he has a better chance of discovering something new in a less hot or fashionable area, and (c) he has a much better chance of being welcomed and appreciated by informants and interviewees in understudied and unfashionable areas.[3]

NOTES

[1] Hall, and Manning quoting Hall, argue that it is the higher status of the physician vis-à-vis the interviewer which is significant in creating this difficulty. Considering successful interviews with judges, congressmen, and important businessmen, I do not think status by itself is the explanatory factor.

[2] I believe people who read both my *How Organizations Are Represented in Washington* (1969) and the section on Congress and lobbyists in *American Business and Public Policy* (although this was published in 1963, all that I wrote of it was completed by late 1955), will see ideas in the new book which should be in the old one, based on interviews conducted for the old one.

[3] There are numerous understudied areas. There are, as yet, relatively few studies in the politics of air and water pollution, for instance, though this will probably change rapidly. Or as Senator Metcalf is fond of pointing out, political scientists have rarely concerned themselves with studying regulatory agencies, federal, state, or Canadian. Or how many sociologists are studying reciprocity, conversation, or resentment? Or how many studies are there of legal counseling or the taking of medical histories?

CHAPTER VI

TOWARD A TRANSACTIONAL THEORY OF INTERVIEWING:

Self-Assessment in the Interview Process

Much of what would otherwise have to be said in this chapter has already been presented by Webb and Salancik in 49 indispensable pages. They show why the reporter-interviewer must develop a self-consciousness about what is affecting the interviewee—including how he himself affects the interviewee.

Of course, assessment of interviewee responses and reactions is as important for other kinds of interviewers as for journalists. Indeed, for the social scientist or for the physician who is taking a medical history, for instance, it ought to be, if anything, more important. They must remember that interviewees, usually, are not engaging in undirected monologues but are, on the contrary, addressing themselves to specific conceptions of a specific audience. And ordinarily conceptions of a specific audience are *in part* determined by the characteristics of the interviewer as perceived by the interviewee.

Webb and Salancik have brought together analytic and experimental evidence to support this finding; however, any interviewer worth his salt intuitively realizes that, for instance, few men will talk in the same way about a job to those whom they regard as not really understanding it as they will to those who strike them as being sophisticated about it. Or interviewers are aware that a question or comment made by a much younger or much older person will often evoke a different kind of response from that made by an age-mate. And so on and so forth—in all elite or specialized interviewing, interviewers will come across many examples of the way in which the interviewer, because of what he is or appears to be, affects the content, the style, the tone of responses. And, similarly, any informant who has had a relationship with the interviewer over a period of time will talk in terms of that particular relationship—not simply indulge in disembodied, abstract responses to abstract stimuli.

What this means is, of course, that whether investigators wish it or not, interviewing is a social relationship and the interviewer is a part of that relationship. The interviewee's *inarticulate and unexamined* conception of the audience guides and determines what he says. A congressman, confronted with a young man who shows eagerness and interest in response to statements about political tactics, may be cued to enlarge on them and to present himself as a political tactician, a realist, the kind of man Frank Kent wrote about in *Political Behavior* or *The Great Game of Politics*. Faced with a different kind of interviewer, this congressman may be cued to present himself as a high-minded public servant. Another congressman, faced successively with the same two interviewers, might be impatient with what he would feel to be a doctrinaire attitude on the part of both, and react in a reverse way—talking in a high-minded fashion to the student interested in political tactics, and trying to shock the other. Now, let us go one step further: without any indication of viewpoint, the mere appearance of one interviewer may make him look like the kind of realist (or behaviorist or cynic, depending on your vocabulary) who is attuned to political tactics whereas the appearance of the other may suggest he is the kind of idealist (or civic-minded person or innocent) who is attuned to expressions of high-minded statesmanship. Or, the name, the sponsorship, the letter of introduction, may lead the interviewee to assign such interpretations. Congressmen, I suspect, in particular—interviewees in general—are fairly shrewd about guessing how interlocutors, including interviewers, play their roles; Charles Horton Cooley long ago explained how such perceptiveness is developed (pp. 66-67). But individual interviewers may have characteristics which to most interviewees or to particular interviewees are in fact misleading; or a particular institutional connection or project description may lead to systematic misinterpretation.

But, in any case, the interviewer tends to affect what is said. Now, there are several ways of trying to get around this situation. First, and most familiar to modern social scientists, is the emphasis upon asking questions *objectively*—that is to say, so managing the impressions one creates that the interviewee has *sup-posedly* no cues to guide him. So long as one is concerned with the kind of social science which Braybrooke describes as being "behavioral" in character, one may be able to rest content with this kind of objectivity. For, in strictly behavioral reporting, one describes only what is clearly available to sensory impression; so-and-so did indeed say this, so-and-so did indeed perform this act at that time under these circumstances. A good deal of survey interviewing, and *some* elite and specialized interviewing, may not need to go any further than this sort of description. However, most elite and specialized interviewing is concerned with what Braybrooke calls "action": it is not sufficient to know that a congressman said a certain thing at a certain time; the analyst wants to know what the remark "meant," how it is to be "interpreted." Now what it means, and the way in which it is to be interpreted, depend as we have just shown upon the context *as perceived by the congressman* within which the remark was uttered. (In other words, cueless interviewing really does not happen.) And since a significant part of that context, for most congressmen under most circumstances, will be created by the interlocutor, the interviewer, this brings the interviewer and the impression he creates right back into the situation. If, for instance, as Congressman Q told me, he was very much annoyed at the survey interview administered to him—and if, as the research assistant who actually administered the schedule told me, he thought that Congressman Q was quite justified in "blowing up" at the superficiality of some of the survey questions—this could be relevant in determining how to interpret what Congressman Q told the interviewer and the meaning and significance of his reported responses. (Indeed, since I was the next person of a scholarly or quasi-scholarly sort to interview Mr. Q, his responses to me for my purposes may have been affected by his recent experience with the other project.) If, as the same assistant implied, Congressman R answered the questions on the schedule somewhat "tongue-in-cheek" to get rid of the whole thing quickly and/or perhaps to please the project director, this also might have affected the meaning and interpretation of responses. Of course, it depends entirely upon the overall purpose of a given study whether such differences in meaning and interpretation matter; all I am saying here is that for many kinds of significant purposes, such differences could matter. Two contrasting cases: if informants were truthful and fairly comprehensive in answering questions on the Grodzins project about federal-state relations, it did not matter much beyond this how they felt about me, the interviewer; but on the Garceau project, which was an effort to find out how businessmen reacted to the "business-in-politics" movement of 1959-60, it could have been quite important to know what role they were taking towards me as an individual and their feelings about being interviewed on such matters. It would have been desirable, too, to assess their conceptions of their obligation to speak in official terms (as representatives of the business firm) or freedom to tell it like it was. For that matter, their attitude towards Harvard University, the sponsoring institution, could have mattered. The fact was that, in general in the Grodzins study, a full set of budgetary figures and reports of attendance at meetings, etc. would have told us most of what we needed to know; interviewing was largely a convenience here, not methodologically a necessity, whereas for the Garceau study it was methodologically necessary.

Unfortunately, in most accounts of interviewing the interviewer suppresses any account of his own role and, except in extreme cases, of interviewee reactions to him. The great advantage of extended direct quotations from the interviewee or informant (and of tape recording) is that it does show—whether the interviewer wishes it or not—to some extent how the interviewee regarded him. And such accounts as Whyte, "The Slum," or Dalton, are very helpful, precisely because they bring the interviewer-investigator into the picture.

Interestingly enough, perhaps the first great interview study —one which, I understand, modern scholars are coming to regard increasingly as highly veridical—did show the interviewer as a significant part of the picture. James Boswell's reports on his discussions with Dr. Johnson show him stimulating and creating situations, much as the modern field interviewer does. Professional and elite interviewers might benefit if someone were to make a careful study of Boswell as interviewer.

But a common reaction to Boswell shows one of the reasons why interviewers do not normally tell us very much about themselves. He is quite often stigmatized as rather laughably egocentric (which indeed he may have been; but his egocentrism enables us to perceive to some degree the stimulus-values he created). The typical scholarly interviewer or taker of a medical history would regard himself as having violated the canons of scholarly decency if he were to tell us about himself in at all the same way that he sometimes tells us about his subjects. For, the general attitude of scholars is that there is "out there" the publicly observable "object" which one is "objectively studying," which is something completely isolated from one's own "subjective" characteristics. Indeed, if recollection serves, I have on several occasions started to try, in analyzing my own interviews, to tell the reader what kind of person I am, how my own characteristics may have affected what the interviewee said (and also, of course, how my own biases might have affected my interpretation of what I thought I heard). But colleagues and editors react by implying that this is egocentric and threatens to waste space on ridiculously subjective matters; so, in fact, I have given up such attempts. (Chapter III above takes a similar risk.)

In fact, in all the literature which is generally classified as political science, and despite the numerous political studies which rely heavily upon interviewing, I do not know of a single case where we are told much about how the interviewer as a person might have affected the product. In a few instances, political scientists *hint* that such knowledge might be useful—for example, Lane, Lasswell, and Salter.[1]

Yet the interviewer is both a part of the situation and the instrument through which recording takes place, and therefore he should be, somehow or other, subject to report. In stressing this point, we are in fact modifying the universal validity or value of the subject-object dichotomy, characteristic of common speech and of the Western tradition in epistemology. Arthur F. Bentley and John Dewey have most clearly challenged the utility of this dichotomy for comprehending social relationships. They have introduced the notion of *transaction*; the person "exists" in a state of dynamic mutual interdependence with other persons and his "personality"—what he says, realizes, and perceives—is a function of this relationship. Raymond Bauer and Ithiel Pool have shown that the audience, as perceived by the "source," helps to determine what the speaker or writer remembers and says and that in this sense the speech or article is a function of the audience as well as of the speaker. Robert Rosenthal has demonstrated in several brilliant experiments that experimenter expectations and teacher expectations do in fact help to determine what experimentee and student produce. Neil Friedman, along the lines pioneered by Rosenthal, tells us:

> Just as the majority of writings on experimentation still have very little to say about the experimenter, so most texts on testing have little to say about the tester, and many reports of therapy have little to say about the therapist. . . . It was through psychological research that unintended social influence was discovered in testing and therapy and now . . . [as witness the title of Rosenthal's contribution, *Experimenter Effects in Behavioral Research*] it is being discovered in research itself [pp. 4-5].

Friedman goes ahead and tells us, *inter alia,* that the social psychologist needs to *discover the stimulus;* he can not simply assume it; and the stimulus may not be at all what he intends it to be or thinks it is (p. 17). And, as he and Rosenthal each suggest, what is regarded as "better" experimentation sometimes is nothing more than teaching the subject to respond to cues the experimenter gives him: the full revolutionary implications of this transactional-social interpretation of psychological experimentation will probably take some years to work out.

But the analogy to the interview situation is clear. The interviewer cannot safely assume that the particular words he uses are in fact the stimulus to which the interviewee is responding. Furthermore, in terms of our knowledge of how role behaviors are varied from situation to situation, it is more reasonable to suppose that the interviewee is reacting to the total set of stimuli which *he perceives in the interview situation* than that he is responding simply to those aspects of it which the interviewer has decided shall be considered as major stimuli. For instance, the interviewer or project director may have decided to ask the congressmen, in the examples given above, specific questions; but the congressmen's interpretation of those questions and "decision" as to how to handle them may depend upon the roles they have "decided" to adopt in the situation, and these roles may be a function of their perceptions of the characteristics of the specific interviewers. Words like "decision" need to be put in quotes here because they imply that there is a conscious process of "thought" about which role to adopt, etc.; more commonly, there is simply a tropism, a response which is not reasoned out at all, but is conditioned by the total situation as felt-and-perceived. Nevertheless, it is more likely that the *total*-situation-as-felt-and-perceived affects or chiefly determines how a respondent answers a set of questions than that he answers these questions in terms of the defined, manifest, and limited meanings which some interviewers think they have. Specific comments and answers, that is, are oftentimes merely items in a general role; and the significant thing in many cases is to know what particular variations of the various roles open to him a respondent is at the moment playing. (See Dean and Whyte in Chapter V above.)

So, interviewers and investigators themselves must—in order to make full sense out of what interviewees and informants say—try to determine how respondents see situations, bearing in mind that the latter's important perceptions may be functions of *un*-analyzed or *un*planned aspects of interviewer behavior. So far as possible, in many situations, the interviewer will no doubt try to control or modify his behavior so as to lead the interviewee to focus attention upon what the investigator has decided in advance to test or study. Success in such an effort is often regarded by scholars as the achievement of "objectivity."[2]

But there is another way of looking at objectivity in the interview, a way which Rosenthal and Friedman have hinted at. Instead of trying to narrow the relationship only to those matters with which the investigator initially was concerned, it often is in the long run more desirable to try to determine what in fact the interviewee or informant was responding to, what he perceived in the situation. Almost certainly, research should alternate between (a) emphasis upon studying and testing responses to a narrowly-defined set of stimuli, with optimum effort to make sure that in actual fact the respondent is responding to the defined stimulus and nothing else and (b) emphasis upon discovering what stimuli are perceived, evoked, dominant to respondents in a given situation. But since there has been less systematic attention to the latter than to the former, it may be well at present to redress the balance by placing emphasis upon the latter. (In any case, some investigators have the kind of imagination and rigor which makes them good at the first, while others may be better at the second.)

Taking this second approach, the task both in the actual interview itself and in later analysis is to try to see what the interviewee is or was reacting to, how he defines the situation. For, as social scientists since the days of W. I. Thomas have asserted, *"definitions of situations" are real social facts* discovery of what the interviewee perceives or believes may in fact yield us social knowledge quite as significant as any obtained from unequivocal responses to unequivocal stimuli. Ambiguities and equivocations, from this point of view, become as significant to the researcher as clear answers to sharply defined questions.

It is important for the interviewer, *during the interview,* to realize what the interviewee is responding to, because on the basis of such realization, he can continuously modify his strategy, formulate his questions, plan his comments. He may even modify his own mannerisms to a limited extent. The skilled interviewer in an unstructured interview, on the basis of the realizations just indicated, can in a very primitive way "test" hypotheses on the run; if he feels that the interviewee is defining the situation in a certain way, is responding to certain stimuli, he asks questions or makes comments designed to get further responses which will test those impressions. As a practical matter, in most studies, interviewers probably do not record most of their intuitions or all efforts to test them, partly because it would be excessively time-consuming to do so, and partly because, although they are operating in terms of "hunches" and hypotheses, the hunches and hypotheses are subconscious and it would be difficult to formulate them. One reason for tape-recording interviews is to permit interviewers, who are so minded, to see if reformulating hypotheses and hunches would enrich understanding. My own hunch is that careful study of a few interviews, after a project has been under way for a few months, would be extremely helpful along this line, and that, at any time, interviewers would profit by formulating their hypotheses about how a given type or class of subject reacts to them. It is also, of course, extremely possible in any two-person relationship that an outsider may be able to see how one or both of them failed to grasp the stimuli to which the other was reacting, so analysis of interviews by third persons may be very valuable.

The Interviewer as a Set of Stimuli

Now, the interviewer is, in the nature of the case, a stimulus or a set of stimuli for the interviewee or informant. The interviewee or informant is also, in the nature of the case, stimuli to the interviewer. And, in the nature of the case, this process of interstimulation may: (a) operate without any formal "objective" relationship to the research problem as initially defined, but (b) be highly significant in determining how interviewers (or those who rely upon their interviews) learn about the problem and interpret what is happening. Let us take an extreme, obviously hypothetical, case: assume an extremely attractive young Negro woman, given to using objective sociological terms like "class," employed in interviewing small businessmen, all white, in border-state cities in 1953 about, for instance, restraint of trade, anti-trust, etc. Suppose, for the moment, they would have talked freely to her; they would certainly have been responding to her characteristics, other than those of being vouched for by a scholarly institution. She might very likely have got results differing in some significant way from those of a middle-aged, unobtrusive, mild-mannered ex-small-town druggist undertaking exactly the same set of interviews. The differences might or might not have mattered for the project; the point is that they could have.

Naturally, there are few cases of interviewers with such a patent tendency to evoke irrelevant stimuli. But I have sometimes wondered whether interviewing by men with academic, not to say pedantic, mannerisms, with a subprofessional or semiprofessional group (policemen, politicians, trade-union leaders) may not be, in fact, just as likely to affect the character of the interview. The point, in general, is not that the Negro girl would necessarily have been sensitive or had a chip on her shoulder, or that pedantic university professors would have been incapable of empathizing with ward heelers; it is simply that, being what they are, they would evoke different role conceptions in enough interviewees to make a difference in the responses.

So far as I know, there is no body of data which would enable us to test this sort of hypothesis at present, because most elite and specialized interview projects have been conducted by only a few people at a time and because the records are not full enough as to what was said, how the interviewer affected interviewees, etc. I may, for instance, guess that a given interviewer appeared rather pedantic to a number of city hall politicians whom he interviewed; but aside from stories about how much he irritated some of them, I have no way of proving the point, or of knowing what proportion of respondents reacted in an irritated fashion. Nor, since we typically get the findings and not the interview reports themselves, is there any way of determining what effect such a reaction might have had on the findings, or whether the interviewer in his analysis took account of it.

In the long run, I suspect that a four-pronged attack is desirable here:

1. We need to work out some way of analyzing selected interviews at some length (partly, perhaps, initially by simulation, or by experiment with students or retired men of prominence, etc.).

2. We need to have published more interviews of years ago. Dollard, for example, tells us that it would be possible to rewrite *Caste and Class in a Southern Town,* placing each item of material in light of the character structure and social position of the informant. "But to do so would be an intolerable breach of trust and in certain cases might endanger my informants" (p. 30). Without any doubt this was true in 1937, when the book was published; but now, in 1969, thirty-two years later, if such rewriting is still possible (Dollard says notes were labeled and information necessary to understand individual informants was available) it is likely, though not certain, that most of the data could decently be published. Similarly, as I have written this

monograph about interviewing, I have come to feel ever more strongly that I ought to publish some of my interview reports on Congress and perhaps on businessmen in Delaware and Cumberland, Maryland, because the findings of Bauer, Pool, and Dexter, based on these interviews, have been widely cited, and because, in a number of cases, the interviewees are dead and so what might have been highly embarrassing in 1954, when the bulk of the interviews were conducted, could now be safely published in some cases. In fact, I have included four interview protocols in *The Sociology and Politics of Congress;* they may be freely regarded as data.

3. Some way should be worked out of comparing interviews and interview reports by different investigators with the same subjects. There have after all been numerous interviews with the same congressman by different scholars; it would be interesting and significant to compare what Representatives Gerald Ford or Richard Bolling or Carl Albert or Wilbur Mills told different scholars, and then, in some cases, go back to the interviewee to discuss discrepancies or problems. This would be particularly helpful, perhaps, when men have retired.[3] Would Senators Gruening or Douglas differently interpret now interviews they conducted then, since they are now out of the Senate?[4]

4. Perhaps most important of all, the interview is after all a two-person relationship, a conversation; but despite all the esoteric topics which social scientists study, there is not a great deal known, apparently, about the sociology of conversation. Work such as that of Lindsey Churchill and Donald E. Allen may enlarge our awareness in this general field, and thereby help understanding of the interview. There are of course many kinds of conversations, which are more like interviews than ordinary conversations but are not interviews, which could profitably be studied; for instance, counseling and negotiation as practiced by lawyers.

Interviewing Skills in Self-Assessment and Empathy

However, the immediately preceding paragraphs are of very little use to the practicing interviewer this year. He is not going to be helped much by speculation about studies which might be conducted someday.

Nevertheless, he can, I believe, profit from the approach just suggested. Essentially, good interviewing is both from the standpoint of practice and that of analysis a matter of perspective. A good interviewer is able to make relevant and applicable guesses, while the interview is going on, as to how he is regarded by the interviewee and to adapt his strategy accordingly; he is able, similarly, to make intelligent guesses about other factors which are affecting the interviewee's choice of role and responses. For instance, a United States senator, interviewed in his home state the week after a successful campaign for re-election is over, may be a somewhat different person from the same man six months later in Washington, who has just been engaged in a bitter committee struggle about what seems to him vital legislation, in which there is little public interest; in the nature of the case, he will probably look at his job differently on the two occasions.

And a good interviewer, also, is aware of his own reactions while the interview is going on and is able almost instantaneously to take account of them. If, for instance, he finds a given interviewee unduly idealistic he may take pains to ask questions which lean a bit in the direction of sympathy with the idealism or he may do the reverse, but he will be aware, and will remember later, which he is doing, and why.

After the interview is completed, when he is writing it up and analyzing it, the good interviewer will take account both of his own reactions and responses and those, so far as he can guess them, of the interviewee. He will, that is, in effect say (to himself if not to his chief), for instance, "the meaning of that statement was . . . to be discounted in this way because of the relationship between us" or, "It was obvious that the interviewee felt very strongly about academic people so perhaps his statements should be evaluated accordingly," or "it may have been that the interviewee's response to me was, for such-and-such reasons, so-and-so, and consequently. . . ."

Much of this has to be done, in most projects, intuitively and subconsciously, certainly without explicit formulation, simply because there is no time to formulate it and write it all out.

This kind of handling of the interview is even more important in journalism and in legal counseling, I would guess, than it is in social science research.

There are not very many documented accounts which show us an interviewer regarding himself as an instrument, analyzing his relationship to interviewees and informants, and generally acquiring perspective. Two highly admirable efforts along this line are by Aaron and by Daniels. Aaron is valuable because he portrays a situation in which it would have been quite impossible for any interviewer to avoid arousing uncertainties, a sense of being threatened, resentment on the part of some interviewee. (It is interesting that most of the reports on oral history studies do not suggest any experiences as intense.)

Aaron was interviewing writers in the 1950's about their leftist activities in the 1930's. He says:

> The historian of the present resembles a hunter stalking his unpredictable quarry in a jungle. . . . In this hunting game, the quarry keeps changing shape. What starts out looking like a rabbit may turn into a porcupine; an elephant is transmogrified into a mouse. To put it still another way: When the investigator tracks down his man . . . some twenty-five to forty-five years after a particular episode, he is not seeing and talking to the same man who wrote the manifesto [etc.] . . . What a person was or did or thought thirty years ago is past and dead, even if that person is technically alive. The living relic is his own ancestor; and feeling a deep, familial piety for his defunct historical self, he indulges in ancestor worship, tidies up embarrassing disorders of his dead past, reverently conceals his own skeleton in a hidden closet . . . [pp. 9-10]. [And even twenty-five minutes later the same thing tends to happen; Philip calm defends Philip angry.]
>
> [And later] . . . These comments on the tangled skein of motives operating invisibly behind the show of events encourages a mistrust any historian feels towards his human subjects. Perhaps they should also awaken a mistrust for his own distorting mind and eye. If the men and women he interviews are guilelessly contributing to the legend of the past how can he be sure that he is not also the inadvertent falsifier . . . unable to divest himself of his own contemporaneity. The "objective" history shades into autobiography . . . [pp. 23-24].

Daniels' account of her experiences as an investigator and interviewer within a military organization gives a brilliant picture of the reactions she seems to have evoked. This report should be read by all self-conscious interviewers, because one sees exactly how what people said to her must have been determined by how she appeared to them, a brash, aggressive young woman, not at all of their sort. One sees that she called senior officers "Colonel, baby," slapped them on their eagles, directed, joked, and generally took an "inappropriate" initiative. She strongly suggests that the way she entered a room affected interview response (p. 278).

There will probably be, at the present time, more general interest in and familiarity with a third great self-assessment by an interviewer-investigator—John Dollard's statements about his biases and roles in working on *Caste and Class In A Southern Town.* "The primary research instrument would seem to be," he declares, "the observing human intelligence, trying to make sense out of the experience. The researcher learns . . . *by fleeting empathy which is followed by reflection and distance* [italics supplied]. He can use a good ear for the overtones in a social situation." Theodore Reik in *Listening with the Third Ear* describes how one may listen for some kinds of overtones, along this line; except for a very brief note by Lane on listening for ideological orientations, and some of Lasswell's work, I do not know of anything which shows or tells the political interviewer, for instance, how to listen for overtones. Yet, the brilliant journalist and the insightful political scientist get good interviews, I would guess, in large measure because they know how to listen for such overtones.

Continuing with Dollard: he says that the investigator notes

> the little clues and contradictions in the statements and behavior of others; jokes made at his expense; the implicit boundaries which guide relationships to others and which oftentimes are not visible until transgressed. . . . To do this type of research, *he must pay the price of intense awareness of self and others* [italics mine], and must constantly attempt to define relationships which are ordinarily taken for granted.

He then proceeds to illustrate how his very efforts to gather life histories and the practical problems arising from racial taboos in finding a place to work with Negro informants in and of itself made clearer some of the central issue of his study.

"The important research act has been exposure and reaction to the social milieu, and a constant attempt to verbalize and organize the ensuing experience." Elite and specialized interviewing, I suspect, only achieves its fullest value when it involves such exposure and subsequent verbalization; I suspect this is even true, for instance, of taking medical histories, *if one really wants to deal with the patient as well as the disease.* I suspect that the fundamental weakness of my effort to undertake a comparative study of state and provincial administrative politics, referred to above (pp. 15-17), was that I tried to undertake interviewing abstractly, independent of much exposure to or knowledge of any given milieu. Whereas, in my studies of Congress and of business in politics, I was sufficiently sensitized to and aware of the milieu, so that I had a handle on interpreting what informants said, and knew how to respond to their initial comments. But it is not by any means certain in advance whether a given milieu will become clear to a given interviewer, whether a given organization is patterned, whether one has enough background to interview usefully—I believe that interviews I conducted about factional conflict in Watertown town meeting politics (the resulting report is as yet unpublished) were valuable, but there was no more reason in advance to feel that I knew enough about Watertown than there was to feel that I knew enough about state administrative politics. One effort worked; the other did not. The moral I draw is that if some initial interviews fail to work out in this way, one should withdraw from or considerably redefine a project.

Still more directly relevant to our central concern with transaction is Dollard's discussion of bias (chap. 3). "It had never occurred to me to consider my own bias until I got into the field." He then tells of an experience with an interviewee who accused him, Dollard, of starting out with a typical northern prejudice. "Returning to my research," he reports, "I found abundant evidence [which is exemplified] of the attitude attributed to me . . ." He then goes ahead and shows how he was led to the realization that "people were forever asking overtly or by implication 'What is this particular Yankee sociologist doing down here?' . . . It finally occurred to me to ask myself: What *was* I doing down there?"

Dollard's discussion of the biases which he discovered in himself in trying to answer this question is particularly valuable because the biases which he discovered were not simple matters of being "for" or "against" something. They rather represented inherent characteristics of the role and self-image which he, as a professional sociologist employed at an elite university, receptive to the intellectually respectable opinions of his time, naturally "had." Most social scientists would, probably, have the same biases today. But they were not only biases which would affect Dollard's interpretation of what he heard and saw. They also created and still create stereotypes in the minds of many informants about what social scientists are like, and therefore they help determine the role informants play towards social scientists.

The biases which he reports are: (a) A strong feeling for the underdog. (This, by the way, is especially characteristic, I think, of sociologists, at least of sociologists who entered the profession prior to 1950. I do not know so many young sociologists and am told that the actuality has shifted; but no doubt the image still lingers on.) (b) "The fact of being a socially mobile person, a member of a middle-class group . . . creates a bias tending to make one's research come out in such a way as to be acceptable to them." Nowadays the precise direction of such a bias would no doubt be different from what it was then; middle-class emphases have shifted. But the general picture is still true; a researcher who ended up with a description, for instance, of Governor Wallace and his supporters which runs quite contrary to the conventional university feeling about them would certainly be risking his career, in a way which would not be the case if he merely demonstrated again the familiar theme that southern Negroes are mistreated. Or a researcher, nowadays, who demonstrated that it is necessary to take quite seriously the belief that behavior can not be materially altered after the age of three or so, and whose work implied therefore that much of the War on Poverty, etc., is likely to be fruitless, would, in many departments and universities, be risking a good deal. Or suppose some study shows the importance of telepathy in interviewing! Now,

of course, there are researchers who are willing to adopt un-
conventional viewpoints of such a nature (see, for comment,
Harwood, or Dexter, *Tyranny*). However, supporters of Governor
Wallace would be quite justified in assuming that social science
researchers as a class are hostile to them, and it would therefore
be natural that they should adopt a different role with social
science researchers than, for instance, supporters of Attorney
General Flowers (the relatively moderate leader in Alabama
politics). Of course, this hypothesis could be tested. (c) Perhaps
no social scientists can escape what Dollard calls "the sociological
bias," the distance from the object of study, an effort to overcome ethnocentrism and a sense of absolute right, a historical
and comparative view of morality and custom. "Taken by itself
this frequently leads to a kind of sociologism which excludes the
biological life altogether." (See Dexter, Heredity.) It is probable
that such a bias would at least lead social science investigators,
as a group, not to think of (and to suppress if they thought of)
questions or comments which evoke genetic or physiological
interpretations of behavior.

Dollard points out, in concluding his analysis of his own biases,
that he discovered them as a result of his research and did not
understand them earlier. But, he says, "if the researcher asks
others to accept his 'intelligence in contact with the data' as a
useful instrument of research . . . there is good reason for turning
about and questioning (this) mental instrument." Equally, let us
stress, since it is the interviewee in contact with *his perceptions*
of the interviewer who provides us with the responses which we
use, we must try to find out what these perceptions are. In the
nature of the case, it will ordinarily happen that an effort to
detect either end of the transactional continuum—the interviewer's biases or the interviewee's perceptions of the interviewer—
will yield some information about the other. But, for best results,
it is desirable, consciously, to consider both ends of the continuum. It is also crucial to remember that though the words
"bias" and "stereotype" are supposed to indicate something bad
(even Dollard speaks half-jocularly of "convicting" other researchers of biases), they are part of the warp and woof of human experience and human relationships. No one has yet dis-

covered any way of relating to others in which they are not present. Yet most researchers fail to discuss their own biases; few scholars since Dollard have tried to emulate, let alone improve upon, his methodological honesty. And, as far as I know, no one has tried to do what Dollard's analysis suggests would be desirable: to develop a chronological history of the development of awarenesses about their own biases, relating such a development to changes in interviewing patterns and observations.

This kind of approach entails the possibility that as one discovers one's own biases or the interviewee's stereotype of problems and issues one may redefine the problem entirely. In some measure, this is what seems to me to have happened (as one who was in touch with it from its inception) in the development of Riesman, Glazer, and Denney's *The Lonely Crowd;* Bateson, in *Naven,* provides perhaps the most sophisticated example of self-conscious self-analysis of the sort which we might more commonly hope for. Logically, what we are talking about here is simply a particular illustration of a general principle: contact with the data may show the scholar that his initial preconceptions about problems and issues demand more or less thoroughgoing revision. But, for our purposes, as interviewers, the data which need to be reconsidered and may be redefined are our own attitudes (biases) and other people's attitudes towards us, matters about which most people are highly sensitive. No doubt, some interviewers would find such reconsideration and possible redefinition a strain;[5] perhaps the best example of a successful effort of this sort was that of a philosopher-turned-journalist, Lincoln Steffens in his *Autobiography.*[6]

The Problematic Nature of the Interview Instrument

We have been concerned here with how we may improve the interview as a tool of data collection. Ultimately, we must deal with problems of inference and "proof." What kinds of conclusions can we draw with what degree of validity from what interviews conducted under what circumstances reported in what fashion? I have not, except in a peripheral fashion, addressed myself to this issue here. This is not because the problem is unimportant; it is rather because it demands careful, reflective study over a period of years, study of a sort which I have not given to it. Cicourel strikes me as going as far as anyone in tackling the matter, especially in his chapter on "Theory and Method in Field Research." It is interesting that he is not (it seems to me) able to carry through as sophisticated an analysis in his following chapter on method and measurement in the sociological *interview*. I suspect that the relative decline in sharpness arises from the simple fact that professional interviewers have, for the most part, assumed without analysis the nature of the process in which they are engaged. Until that process is itself viewed as problematic, something to be analyzed and explored, we will not be ready to determine what it records and measures, let alone how it can be used to draw valid inferences, etc. Cicourel had, that is, to try to make bricks with very little straw.

It is much as though we were relying for our knowledge of some Platonic cave upon a machine which *somehow* took something like that we nowadays call photographs. But if no one had any clear idea as to what the process was by which the pictures developed—if independent tests of their accuracy were extremely fragmentary and not comparable with each other—if there was no worked-out theory even as to why the pictures happened to be recorded on the recording mechanism—indeed, if, for all any one knew for sure, *some* of the pictures were simply pictures of wandering currents of air, so replicated as to seem like the people inside a cave, whereas others were veridical representations —then the most pressing need would be to improve knowledge and theory about how the machine worked. Simultaneously, of course, one would hope to tackle the issue of valid inference.

In the meantime, as Webb and Salancik make clear through the title of their monograph, "The Interview or The Only Wheel In Town," even though we need to clarify the process by which interviews work much more than has been done, it is still true that interviewing is for many purposes the best or the only source of insight that we have, insecure as it sometimes is.

Now for many interviewers—as indeed for me personally for many years—this sort of discussion is largely unnecessary. Just as many medical researchers do not need to be bothered with problems of the language of science, so many skillful specialized interviewers can operate satisfactorily enough with practical approaches of the sort sketched in the preceding chapters here and in Webb and Salancik. And, in Bentley's words on a comparable matter (*Behavior*, p. 183):

> To any one whose tasks can be performed on such a ground, I have not the slightest thought of bringing disturbance. But for many of us tasks are pressing in the course of which our firmest spots of conventional departure [such as subject-object isolationality] themselves dissolve in function. When they have so dissolved, and when we are so involved, there is no hope of finding refuge in some chance island of "fact" which may appear. The continents go, and the islands. The pang may be like that felt by a confirmed landsman at his first venture on the ocean, but the ocean in time becomes familiar and secure. Or, if I may change the figure, the fledgling will vastly prefer his firm nest to falling with untried wings. But the parent sciences are pushing; the nest, even, is disintegrating; and there is air for flight, even though it is not so vividly felt and seen as the sticks and straws of the nest.

NOTES

[1] Ironically enough, Arthur F. Bentley, whose *Process of Government* (1908), has often been hailed as the first successful effort in modern behavioral political science, in later years, more than any other scholar, tried to break down the notion that individuals could be satisfactorily studied *as such*, and that the data could be divorced from the investigator—see, for instance, "The Human Skin: Philosophy's Last Line of Defense," in his *An Inquiry Into Inquiries*, pp. 195-211, and "Situational vs. Psychological Theories of Behavior," *ibid.*, pp. 141-74, and also "Isolationality: Language and Fact," in *Behavior, Knowledge, Fact*, pp. 105-11. But Bentley's later work was ignored by the political science profession, insofar as I know.

A careful student of the complete works of Charles E. Merriam, the other founder of modern American realistic political science, would no doubt find clues and cues here and there to the background and the personality which led to his observations. But, sadly enough, most people who did not know him will find these volumes, in large part, dull, because Merriam the politician, Merriam the observer, Merriam the very vain, Merriam who interacted with his data, is almost   entirely missing—yet this Merriam could be and was in private conversation instructive and fascinating. But it was Merriam as what he regarded as a gossip, Merriam the raconteur, who was instructive; Merriam the writer, by cutting out that "other" Merriam, often became pedantic.

The literary and impressionistic emphasis upon subjectivity is, of course, as misleading as the scholarly emphasis upon being hyper-objective. But, as a corrective to the scholarly emphasis, note Oriana Fallaci's statement in her report on the space program, *If the Sun Dies:* "This book is ruthlessly autobiographical. . . . This raises the question whether I have been objective or not. The reply is that I have not been; I do not believe in objectivity. . . . Within conscience or memory, objectivity can not exist. . . . A true portrait of a man cannot be achieved without the beliefs, the feelings, the tastes of the painter" (p. vii).

[2] There is a considerable parallel between this "objective" approach to interviewing and the teaching situation. A great deal of teaching, obviously, consists of directing the student to give answers of a sort which take into account only a limited range of variables and to leave out of account everything else. Interviewing is merely a continuation of this; Daniel Lerner (1958) tells us of Turks who simply could not answer questions about what they would do if they were in positions of high authority; they could not leave out of account the fact that indeed they did not occupy such posts (pp. 3, 51, 141-44). But, sufficiently well tutored by Lerner and subsequent generations of interviewers, and much more by the experience of schooling, younger generations of Turks are becoming increasingly good subjects for survey interviews.

In effect, what the school does, and what the survey interviewer or equivalent does, is to try to teach the student or respondent to accept what is regarded as an appropriate doctrine of *relevance*. The ability to draw hard, definite lines between the "relevant" and the "ir-relevant" is of tremendous value for some purposes and should cer-tainly be part of the process of modernizing education; but it is highly questionable whether in most elite or specialized interviewing it is helpful to persuade interviewees to accept the interviewer's definition of relevance—for, not infrequently, some thing which the interviewer starts out by regarding as *ir*relevant may turn out to be highly relevant in interpreting the interviewee's actions and attitudes. In fact, the history of discovery in sociology and political science could be largely organized as a history of the awareness of new criteria of relevance. (See Schiller on the doctrine of relevance.)

[3] I have an example from my own experience as interviewee. Daniel Elazar in *American Federalism: A View from the States* (New York:

Crowell, 1966), p. 73, quotes me as saying that Governor Foster Furcolo effectively reorganized the office of "state representative" in Washington, and that I said so on September 9, 1957. I know the assertion was not true; I was shocked to read it; I even have no recollection of being interviewed on the project on September 9, 1957; but I suspect I was not misunderstood. I suspect that, whatever the circumstances, they were ones which elicited from me the formal line of the Furcolo administration with which I was at that date connected; if I had been queried at a somewhat later date, after I had left the Furcolo administration entirely, I would have made clear there was no genuine reorganization, simply a lot of purely ritual talk.

⁴ It would also be valuable to collate interviews conducted with the same interviewee when occupying different positions—for example, with Congressman Bolling when a confidante of Speaker Rayburn's as compared with what he says when he is a prominent critic of Speaker McCormack's; with *Congressman* Eugene McCarthy, with *Senator* Eugene McCarthy, and then with *ex-presidential candidate* Eugene McCarthy. There have been various striking changes in community attitude and orientation; biographies and political histories show us, of course, how men change; there are collections of letters by nineteenth-century politicians which could be analyzed to show changing role perceptions over time; but analysis of interviews taken over time would add a new dimension.

⁵ It may appear that I am somewhat critical of my colleagues in regard to the way many of them conduct interviews. To the extent this is true, all I can say is that I too am guilty. I started interviewing in a supposedly professional fashion in 1937 (the interviews which resulted in Dexter, "Administration"), and it took me fifteen years to begin to realize any of the major points made in this chapter. In subsequent years I was employed as an interviewer for military intelligence purposes on a joint project of the Board of Economic Warfare and the Office of Strategic Services on such matters as the political situation in North Africa; I conducted two efforts to determine the effects of a religious conference on the expressed attitudes of those who attended it, which resulted in two published articles; I directed interviewers and myself interviewed for the Katona project; I did political interviewing, designed to aid in the selection of a candidate for congress (and which in fact did lead to the selection of a previously unthought-of candidate by the organization); I interviewed a number of people in his district and in Washington on John Taber's record as a congressman (see Dexter "John Taber"); and I interviewed several hundred specialists in the field of retardation on how to spend trust moneys left for the benefit of the retarded. But

in all this interviewing I never became conscious of the fact that the process of interviewing itself is a social phenomenon, which can profitably be analyzed reflectively. I never *thought* about it, any more than I thought about the way I walk or how to make my heart beat better.

When I started the trade study in the fall of 1953, 18 years after I had entered graduate school, I was, intellectually speaking, just as naive about conducting and evaluating interviews as I had been in 1935. Practically speaking, of course, I was a better interviewer because I had had more experience and knew more about a good many fields. But, by the time the trade study interviews were completed, in the spring of 1955, I had, somehow or another, developed a conscious theory of how to interview and how to assess and evaluate interviews—a theory which, I think, I have improved since, but which, in general, rough terms, was preliminary to this book.

It would have been desirable, from the standpoint of a study of self-consciousness in interviewing, if I had thought to make a detailed record of how I responded to different interviews in the trade study, and why; of course, that was not the objective of the trade study, and I cannot very well reconstruct now what stimuli affected me then. One important factor probably was that I was personally more interested and involved in the trade study than in any previous study which I had done; another was the encouragement by my colleagues, Raymond Bauer and Ithiel Pool, to think about the interview process. So far as I can now recollect, I happened by sheer chance in the fall of 1953 to pick up a copy of Theodore Reik's *Listening with the Third Ear*, and I felt that this opened a new viewpoint towards interviewing to me. But why had I not seen anything special in Dollard's book, which I had read a number of times without realizing it bore upon me as an interviewer? Or I had long been accustomed to using Kenneth Burke's *Attitudes toward History* as a source of insight and understanding; yet, until after I developed a theory of interviewing, I did not see that, for example, some of his notions (e.g., on "cues," pp. 236-43 and "discounting," pp. 244-46) were highly relevant to my interviews. I think that the 1954 issuance in collected form of the later papers of Arthur F. Bentley, who had been a particular intellectual stimulus to me, made me more aware at that time of the notion of transaction as basic in all social relationships, even interviewing. And I am inclined to suppose that my study and use, from 1947 to 1950, of Nathaniel Cantor's *Dynamics of Learning* in connection with my teaching then must have had an influence on my interviewing; at any rate, retrospectively, I can see a close relationship between some aspects of his theory of the teaching process and my emphases in interviewing.

[6] Or I had better say that Steffens provides a particularly successful and self-conscious example of a picture of changing perspectives in autobiography; I suspect that the most successful examples, most valuable for interviewers, of what is here talked about may be found in novels. The main theme of the very popular *My Friend* series by Jane Duncan might well be described as that of how the perspective of the writer changes with changing situations and evaluations. In default of reading the whole series (recommended), perhaps the two where her changing self-assessments are most obvious are *My Friends, The Macleans* and *My Friends, The Mrs. Millers.*

REFERENCES AND SOURCES

This is in no way a comprehensive bibliography; it merely lists the works to which I have referred in the text and those which I am sure I would refer to were I to teach a course in interviewing or in counseling and negotiation, or in the taking of medical histories, or the like. Since there is no bibliography on elite and specialized interviewing—and some readers may want to use this listing as a partial substitute—I have added annotations in a number of cases.

In view of the lack of such a bibliography, readers will find Webb and Salancik indispensable, and Richardson, Dohrenwend, and Klein very useful as bibliographic guides. There is also an extremely well-chosen "Selected Bibliography for Methods of Field Work" in Powdermaker, pp. 307-11; unfortunately, it is not annotated, nor are most of the cited works discussed in her text.

The best way of familiarizing oneself with different approaches to problems of interviewing and, especially, of the use of informants, is probably to look through the files of *Human Organization* (formerly *Applied Anthropology*). A number of articles in *The Public Opinion Quarterly* are also pertinent, although these tend to be concerned with the survey rather than with the elite or specialized interview. I located a number of additional, helpful references from *Sociological Abstracts*; somewhat to my surprise, I did not turn up anything further of use from either *Psychological Abstracts* or *International Political Science Abstracts.*

For reference to a checklist of sources dealing with interviewing for fact, see below under Dexter, "untitled paper."

Aaron, Daniel. "The Treachery of Recollection; The Inner and Outer History." In *Essays on History and Literature,* edited by R. H. Bremner, pp. 3-27. Columbus: Ohio State University Press, 1966.

Abrahamson. See Fenlason.

Allen, Donald E., Oklahoma State University, Stillwater (Department of Sociology), is engaged in a study of the manifest behavior sequences in two-person conversation in an effort to illuminate the components and dynamics of such conversation. He is developing a system of categorizing elements in conversations which might be helpful in analyzing the interview.

Altick, R. *The Scholar Adventurers.* New York: Macmillan, 1950. See "Hunting for Manuscripts," pp. 86-121.

Anton, Thomas. *The Politics of State Expenditures in Illinois.* Urbana, Ill.: University of Illinois Press, 1966.

Back, Kurt W., and Kenneth J. Gergen. "Idea Orientation and Ingratiation in the Interview: A Dynamic Model of Response Bias." *Proceedings of the Social Statistics Section, American Statistical Association, 1963,* pp. 284-88.

Barnes, I. A. "Some Ethical Problems of Modern Fieldwork." *British Journal of Sociology,* XIV (1963), 118-33.

Bartlett. See Nadel; Lindgren.

Bateson, G. *Naven.* Cambridge: Cambridge University Press, 1936, pp. 257-80.

His account of his problems in struggling with the data, "deciding" what to record, etc., is quite stimulating but extremely difficult to follow.

Bauer, Raymond. "The Audience." In *Handbook of Communications*. Chicago: Rand McNally, forthcoming.

_____. "The Communicator and His Audience." In *People, Society, and Mass Communications*, edited by L. Dexter and D. Whyte, pp. 125-40. New York: Free Press, 1964. Reprinted with editorial comment from *Journal of Conflict Resolution*, Vol. II (1958).

_____. "The Obstinate Audience." *American Psychologist*, XIX (1964), 319-28.

These three articles by Bauer develop most clearly the empirical evidence for the notion that it is desirable or even essential to regard relationships between the source and those-communicated-to as transactional rather than as one-way matters. The present book on interviewing is, among other things, an attempt to apply that notion to the interview.

Bauer, Raymond, Ithiel de Sola Pool, and Lewis A. Dexter. *American Business and Public Policy*. New York: Atherton, 1963.

Beattie, John. *Understanding an African Kingdom: Bunyoro*. New York: Holt, Rinehart and Winston, 1965.

Beattie is helpful because he shows how he prepared himself and how he tried out different ways of gathering data. Along with Whyte, this should be read by anyone desiring to know how interviewing and the use of informants is related to other ways of getting data. Political scientists will probably find this report more valuable than most sociological or anthropological reports on field techniques because Africanists, more than most anthropologists, have long had an interest in political process, an interest which shows up here.

Becker, Howard S. "Problems in the Publication of Field Studies." In *Reflections on Community Studies*, edited by A. Vidich, J. Bensman, and M. Stein, pp. 267-84.

A judicious discussion, somewhat broader in implications

than the title indicates, of ethical problems involved in research.

Becker, Theodore. "Surveys and Judiciaries: or Who's Afraid of the Purple Curtain." *Law and Society Review*, I (1966), 133-43.

Benney. See Riesman.

Bensman. See Vidich.

Bentley, Arthur F. *Behavior, Knowledge, Fact*. Bloomington, Ind.: Principia Press, 1935.

————. *An Inquiry into Inquiries*. Boston: Beacon Press, 1954.

These two volumes by Bentley provide the best statement of the way in which to approach human behavior transactionally. However, they are dense and so abstract as to be lacking in much excitement or stimulus to imagination. See also Dewey.

Best, Gary Lee. "Diplomacy in the United Nations." Ph.D. dissertation, Northwestern University, August, 1960.

Cited by Jacobson.

Biddle. See Robinson.

Biderman. See Dexter.

Bingham, W., B. Moore, and J. Gustad. *How to Interview*. 4th rev. ed. New York: Harper, 1959.

Bobrow. See Dexter.

Boswell, James. *Life of Samuel Johnson*. Of which there are many editions.

Boswell is, of course, chiefly famous for his extensive "interviews" with Johnson, which deserve study by someone familiar with twentieth-century interviewing practice and theory. Our knowledge of how he *worked*—and the term is used advisedly—has been much reinforced by Professor Pottle's reconstruction of his other writings: see, for example, C. Ryskamp and F. Pottle, eds., *Boswell: The Ominous Years, 1774-1776* (New York: McGraw-Hill, 1963), pp. 345 ff., for an account which most anthropologists might well envy. Boswell, indeed, should be studied along with Webb, Campbell, Schwarz, and Sechrest as a stimulus to the imagination.

Braybrooke, David. *Philosophical Problems of the Social Sciences.* New York: Macmillan, 1965. Introduction.

Bremner. See Aaron.

Bright. See Kincaid.

Brooks, Philip C. In *Oral History at Arrowhead,* edited by E. Dixon and J. V. Mink, pp. 5-11.

Brown, Robert. *Explanation in Social Science.* Chicago: Aldine, 1963.

Most interviewing is designed to help get something "explained," but Brown makes it clear that we can profitably study what we mean by "explain." See also Sjoberg and Nett on explanation.

Buchanan. See Wahlke.

Bucher, Rue, Charles E. Fritz, and E. L. Quarantelli. "Tape Recorded Interviews in Social Research." *American Sociological Review,* XXII (1956), 359-64.

————. "Tape Recorded Research: Some Field and Data Processing Problems." *Public Opinion Quarterly,* XX (1956), 427-39.

Burke, Kenneth. *Attitudes toward History*. 2d rev. ed. Boston: Beacon Press paperback, 1961.

Although there is only one explicit reference to this discussion in my text, Burke's approach to interpretation of terms does, I believe, enrich the theory of interviewing I develop; so far as I can trace my own intellectual history, at any rate, Bentley's notion of transaction and Burke's theory of interpretation (as here set forth; I have not found anything useful for our purposes in his later work) have been major influences in developing my ideas.

Campbell. See Webb, E.

Cantor, Nathaniel. *Dynamics of Learning*. 3d ed. Buffalo: Foster & Stewart, 1946.

The theoretical approach to learning and teaching sociology is quite similar to mine toward research in interviewing.

Caplow, Theodore. "Dynamics of Information Interviewing." *American Journal of Sociology*, LXII (1956-57), 165-71.

Some interesting hypotheses about the satisfactions interviewees get from the experience.

Carroll. See Gray.

Casagrande, Joseph B. *In The Company of Man*. New York: Harper, 1960.

Describes informants used by a number of different anthropologists. (No similar study of informants in modern societies is known to me—suppose Lasswell, Salter, Hunter, and various students of Congress gave us similar portrayals!)

Chaplin, David. "Interviewing Foreign Elites." Mimeographed. Presented at American Sociological Association, 1968.

Chaplin, who is in the Department of Sociology, University

of Wisconsin, is preparing a book on interviewing foreign elites, developing this paper.

Churchill, Lindsey. "Investigation of Information Exchange and Questions." Research project under way at Russell Sage Foundation (January, 1969).

Cicourel, Aaron. *Method and Measurement in Sociology.* New York: Free Press, 1964. Chiefly Chapters II ("Theory and Methods in Field Research") and III ("Interviewing"), but see also IX ("Language and Meaning") and X ("Theoretical Presuppositions").

Colvard, R. "Interaction and Identification in Reporting Field Research: A Critical Consideration of Protective Procedures." In *Ethics, Politics, and Social Research,* edited by Gideon Sjoberg, pp. 319-38.

Should be read in connection with Vidich and Bensman, 1964, and Dexter on jeopardy. Colvard suggests a number of penetrating questions about the obligation to protect the privacy of the interviewee, and the way in which this may degenerate into a procedure to protect the scholar himself against warranted criticism; he also calls attention to the scholar's obligation to specify so that rechecking of data is possible.

Cook. See Jahoda.

Cooley, Charles Horton. *Social Organization.* New York: Scribner, 1929, pp. 66-67.

Explains how facial expression may come to be a recognizable concomitant of role, status, and orientation.

Crane. See Hunt.

Dalton, Melville. *Men Who Manage; Fusions of Feeling and Theory in Administration.* New York: Wiley, 1959. Appendix on Method, pp. 273-85.

A sophisticated and convincing account of the usefulness and, for some problems, necessity of covert, masked research.

Daniels, Arlene K. "The Low Caste Stranger in Social Research." In *Ethics, Politics, and Social Research,* edited by Gideon Sjoberg, pp. 267-96.

Davis, Allison, Burleigh Gardner, and Mary Gardner. *Deep South: A Social-Anthropological Study of Caste and Class.* Chicago: University of Chicago Press, 1941.

One of the relatively few studies where it was decided in advance that the same investigator-interviewers could not cover the different groups in a community, so Negroes studied Negroes and whites studied whites. Nothing is said (except for pp. viii-ix) on interviewing technique.

Dean, John P. "Participant Observation and Interviewing." In *Introduction to Social Research,* edited by John Doby, pp. 225-52. Harrisburg, Pa.: Stackpole, 1954.

Dean, John P., and William Foote Whyte. "How Do You Know the Informant Is Telling the Truth?" Reprinted here in Chapter V.

Denney. See Riesman.

Deutsch, Karl W. *Arms Control and the Atlantic Alliance.* New York: Wiley, 1967.

Deutsch, M. See Jahoda.

Dewey, John, and Arthur F. Bentley. *Knowing and the Known.* Boston: Beacon Press, 1954.

Develops the notion and meaning of transaction as a key

approach to observing social phenomena. This book on interviewing is essentially a transactional theory of the interview;
Friedman and Rosenthal provide us with transactional
theories of experimentation.

Dexter, Lewis A. "Administration of the Social Gospel." *Public
Opinion Quarterly*, II (1938), 294-99.

_____. "Civil Defense Viewed As a Problem of Innovation."
Mimeographed. Oak Ridge, Tenn.: Oak Ridge National
Laboratory, 1966.

_____. "Congressmen and the Formulation of Military Policy."
In *New Perspectives on Congress,* edited by R. Peabody
and N. Polsby. 2d ed. Chicago: Rand McNally, 1969. Also
in *Components of Defense Policy,* edited by D. Bobrow.
Chicago: Rand McNally, 1965. And in *A Reader in American
Government,* edited by M. Irish, J. Prothro, and R. Lineberry. Englewood Cliffs, N. J.: Prentice-Hall, 1969.

_____. "Congressmen and the People They Listen To." Dittoed.
Center for International Studies, Massachusetts Institute of
Technology, 1955. (Out of print, but available at the Library
of Congress and other major libraries.) Also Ph.D. dissertation, Columbia University, 1959. A drastic condensation
appears in Bauer, Pool, and Dexter.

_____. "The Good Will of Important People: More on the
Jeopardy of the Interview." *Public Opinion Quarterly,* XXVII
(1964), 556-63.

_____. "Heredity and Environment Reexplored: Specification
of Environments and Genetic Transmission." *Eugenics
Quarterly,* III (1956), 88-94.

_____. *How Organizations Are Represented in Washington.*
Indianapolis: Bobbs-Merrill, 1969.

Largely based upon interviews with association representatives, congressmen, etc.

————. "John Taber: Watchdog of the Treasury." *Zion's Herald* (Boston), August 1, 1948.

————. "More on Voter's Information About Candidates." *P.R.O.D.* (now *American Behavioral Scientist*), I (1958), 36-38.

————. "On Interviewing Business Leaders." *P.R.O.D.* (now *American Behavioral Scientist*), II (1959), 25-29.

"In fact, much of interviewing value can be obtained by appealing to the executive to teach you, *the subordinate*," remembering that "the scholar is to them ordinarily a subordinate." Suggests that the problems of Kincaid and Bright may have arisen from an effort to direct the interview. (Incidentally, it is probable that the superordinate-subordinate relationship between businessmen and scholars is not as clear now as it was in 1958 when the article was written.) This is unique in the literature, so far as I know, as being the only criticism directed against a report on interviewing as a method of data collecting in terms of interviewing theory!

————. "On the Use and Abuse of Social Science by Practitioners." *American Behavioral Scientist*, IX (1965), 25-29.

————. "Role Relationships and Conceptions of Neutrality in Interviewing." *American Journal of Sociology*, LXII (1956), 153-57.

————. *The Sociology and Politics of Congress.* Chicago: Rand McNally, 1970.

Includes in Appendix B protocols of four interviews conducted for the trade study with: the late Samuel Jacobs, legislative assistant to the late Senator Patrick McNamara (Michigan); former Congressman Victor Knox (Michigan); the late Congressman Cleveland Bailey (West Virginia); the late Congressman Thomas Jenkins (Ohio). These protocols are, in a limited degree, data for this current book on elite interviewing.

————. *Tyranny of Schooling: An Inquiry into the Problem of "Stupidity."* New York: Basic Books, 1964.

————. Untitled paper on interviewing for fact. Prepared for the Bureau of Social Science Research, Washington, D.C., Albert Biderman, project director. Accompanied by a bibliography of some 50 titles not listed herein. This paper was based upon an earlier report by Raymond Fink. This may shortly be available in mimeographed form.

Dexter, Lewis A., and David M. White, eds. *People, Society, and Mass Communications.* New York: Free Press, 1964.

Dickson. See Roethlisberger.

Dixon, Elizabeth, and James V. Mink, eds., *Oral History at Arrowhead: The Proceedings of the First National Colloquium in Oral History.* Mimeographed, 1967. Available from Knox Mellon, Treasurer, Oral History Association (Department of History, Immaculate Heart College, 2021 N. Western Avenue, Los Angeles, California 90027), $3.00.

See Brooks, Starr, and Morrissey for cited material. See discussion of best interviewer (p. 40), preparation of interviewer comments (p. 41), autobiography versus interviewing (pp. 44-48), conceivable technologies in interviewing (pp. 59-60), and interviewing of psychiatrists (pp. 78-93).

Doby. See Dean.

Dohrenwend. See Richardson.

Dollard, John. *Caste and Class in a Southern Town.* New Haven: Yale University Press, 1937. See Chapter II ("Research Method") and Chapter III ("Bias").

Indispensable.

Duncan, Jane. *My Friends, the Macleans.* New York: St. Martin's Press, 1967.

————. *My Friends, the Mrs. Millers.* New York: St. Martin's Press, 1964.

Elazar. See Gray; Grodzins.

Eulau. See Wahlke.

Fallaci, Oriana. *If the Sun Dies.* New York: Athenaeum, 1966, pp. vii-ix.

Fenlason, Anne F. *Essentials in Interviewing for the Interviewer Offering Professional Services.* 2d ed., rev. by G. Ferguson and A. Abrahamson. New York: Harper, 1962.

Although some social scientists may find this a bit naive, it has, nevertheless, useful practical suggestions which are not clearly stated elsewhere.

Ferguson, G. See Fenlason.

Ferguson, L. See Wahlke.

Fink. See Dexter.

Fiske, See Merton.

Friedman, Neil. *The Social Nature of Psychological Research.* New York: Basic Books, 1967.

Fritz. See Bucher.

Garceau, O., and C. Silverman. "A Pressure Group and the Pressured." *American Political Science Review,* XLVIII (1954), 672-91.

Gardner, B. See Davis.

Gardner, M. See Davis.

Gergen. See Back.

Glaser, Barney, and Anselm Strauss. *The Discovery of Grounded Theory.* Chicago: Aldine, 1967. See "Library Materials: Advantages and Limitations," pp. 176-83; "Insight and Theory Development," pp. 251-57.

Glazer. See Riesman.

Glick, H. R. "Interviewing Judges: Access and Interview Setting." In *Research Reports in Social Science, Institute for Social Research.* Tallahassee: Florida State University, February, 1970.

One of the few reports which gives detailed accounts of the two variables, access and interview setting.

Goldner, Fred. "Role Emergence and the Ethics of Ambiguity." In *Ethics, Politics, and Social Research,* edited by Gideon Sjoberg, pp. 245-66.

This can profitably be read in connection with the article by Daniels in the same volume. It also provides a basis for developing an aspect of the transactional theory of the interview not treated in my text—the way in which, as in other social interactions, interviewer-observer-investigator and interviewed-observed-investigated may be feeling each other out to reach an adequately satisfying role relationship. Relates to Donald E. Allen's research, I think.

Gorden, Raymond L. *Interviewing: Strategy, Technique, and Tactics.* Homewood, Ill.: Dorsey Press, 1969.

Came out after this book was completed. It covers much ground; see my review in the *American Sociological Review,* in press.

Gray, Kenneth. "Congressional Interference in Administration." In *Cooperation and Conflict: A Reader on American Federalism,* edited by Daniel Elazar, R. Carroll, J. Levine, and D. St. Angelo, pp. 521-42. Itasca, Ill.: F. E. Peacock, 1969.

Grey, David. "Interviewing at the [Supreme] Court." *Public Opinion Quarterly,* XXXI (1967), 285-89.

Grimshaw, Allen D. "Language as Obstacle and Data in Sociological Inquiry." *Items,* XXIII (1969), 17-26.

I have been particularly impressed with this report, especially by the leads suggested on the ethnography of questioning.

Grodzins, Morton. *The American System.* Edited by Daniel Elazar. Chicago: Rand McNally, 1966.

Gross, Neal, and Ward Mason. "Some Methodological Problems of Eight-Hour Interviews." *American Journal of Sociology,* LXIX (1953-54), 197-204.

Largely reproduced in N. Gross, W. Mason, and A. McEachern, *Explorations in Role Analysis* (New York: Wiley, 1958), pp. 85-90. Particularly helpful where the would-be interviewer has prestige from the standpoint of the prospective interviewee.

Gusfield, J. R. "Field Work Reciprocities in Studying a Social Movement." *Human Organization,* XIV (1955), 29-33.

One of the most valuable articles.

Gustad. See Bingham.

Hall, Oswald. "The Informal Organization of Medical Practice." Ph.D. dissertation (sociology), University of Chicago, 1944.

————. "Types of Medical Careers." *American Journal of Sociology,* LV (1950), 243-53.

Hall, R. L., and C. J. Hitch. "Price Theory and Business Behavior." *Oxford Economic Papers,* no. 2. London: Oxford University Press, May, 1939, pp. 12-45.

Especially see the Appendix, which summarizes what are apparently interview results on pricing policy.

Harrison, Paul M. *Authority and Power in the Free Church Tradition: A Social Case Study of the American Baptist Convention.* Princeton, N.J.: Princeton University Press, 1959.

Harrisson. See Mass-Observation.

Harwood, Edwin. "The Basic Itch." *American Sociologist,* III (1968), 248.

Hayakawa, S. I. *Language in Thought and Action.* 2d ed. New York: Harcourt, Brace, 1964. Especially see the section in Chapter 3 on "Discovering One's Bias."

Heard, Alexander. "Interviewing Southern Politicians." *American Political Science Review,* XLIV (1950), 886-96. See also Key.

Hitch. See Hall.

Holmstrom, Engin E. "Information or Noise." Mimeographed, ONR 1181(11), Project NR 177-470, Technical Report no. 18, Duke University, September, 1965. Based upon Ph.D. dissertation (sociology).

Hunt, Wm. H., Wilder W. Crane, and John C. Wahlke. "Interviewing Political Elites in Cross-Cultural Comparative Research." *American Journal of Sociology,* LXX (1964), 59-68.

A very much longer version in mimeographed form was still available in 1968 from the individual authors.

Hunter, Floyd. *Community Power Structure.* Chapel Hill: University of North Carolina Press, 1953.

Irish. See Dexter.

Isaacs, Harold. *Scratches on Our Minds: American Images of China and Japan.* New York: John Day, 1958.

At one time, I intended to include in this book a considerable portion of the Introduction (pp. 11-35), which describes how Isaacs set about selecting interviewees and approaching them. Reasons of space, as well as an increasing sense that the scientific common sense of the introduction is more thoroughly apparent after reading the report on the entire study, finally decided me not to do so.

Jacobson, Harold K. "Deriving Data from Delegates to International Assemblies: A Research Note." *International Organization,* XXI (1967), 592-613.

Jacobson, L. See Rosenthal.

Jahoda, M., M. Deutsch, and S. Cook, eds. *Research Methods in Social Relations.* New York: Dryden, 1951. Notably the section on Selected Techniques, pp. 424-62. (Later editions have listed C. Selltiz as senior editor.)

Jastak, J., H. MacPhee, and M. Whiteman. *Mental Retardation, Its Nature and Incidence: A Population Survey of the State of Delaware.* Newark, Del.: University of Delaware Press, 1963.

Kahn. See Katz.

Katona, George. *Price Control and Business: Field Studies among Producers and Distributors of Consumer Goods in the Chicago Area, 1942-1944.* Bloomington, Ind.: Principia Press, 1945.

Katz, Daniel, and Robert Kahn. *The Social Psychology of Organizations.* New York: Wiley, 1966.

See the review of this book by L. A. Dexter in *American Political Science Review,* LXII (1968), 1306-7.

Kendall. See Merton.

Kent, Frank. *The Great Game of Politics*. Garden City, N.Y.: Doubleday, 1923.

_____. *Political Behavior*. New York: Morrow, 1928.

Key, V. O., with the assistance of Alexander Heard. *Southern Politics in State and Nation*. New York: Knopf, 1949. See also Heard.

Kincaid, H. W., and M. Bright. "Interviewing the Business Elite." *American Journal of Sociology*, LXIII (1957), 304-11.

For a criticism of this, see Dexter, "On Interviewing Business Leaders."

Klein. See Richardson.

Kroeber. See Paul.

Lane, Robert E. *Political Ideology: Why the American Common Man Believes What He Does*. New York: Free Press, 1962.

Among political science documents, this is unquestionably the best argument against the necessity (which I argue for in this book) of reporting on the interviewer as well as on the interviewee; it is, however, ironic that Lane, who expresses his profound acknowledgment to Dollard and to Reik, does not follow their procedure and tell us about himself.

Lasswell, Harold D. *Democracy through Public Opinion*. Menasha, Wis.: George Banta Publishing Co., 1941. See "Know Thyself," pp. 44-60.

_____. *Power and Personality*. New York: Viking Press, 1962. See "Varieties of Character and Personality," pp. 62-93.

_____. *Psychopathology and Politics*. Chicago: University of Chicago Press, 1930.

This is largely based upon interviews of a psychoanalytic character, and discusses their use as a research tool.

Lazarsfeld, Paul F., and Wagner Thielens, Jr. *The Academic Mind*. New York: Free Press, 1958.

Lerner, Daniel. "Interviewing Frenchmen." *American Journal of Sociology*, LXII (1956-57), 187-94.

_____. *The Passing of Traditional Society: Modernizing the Middle East*. New York: Free Press, 1958.

Particularly valuable because of its picture of the different problems involved in interviewing what are called transitionals, traditionals, and moderns (but see Riesman's Introduction).

Levin, Murray. *The Compleat Politician: Political Strategy in Massachusetts*. Indianapolis: Bobbs-Merrill, 1962.

Levine. See Gray.

Lewis, Wilmarth Sheldon. *Collector's Progress*. New York: Knopf, 1951.

_____. *One Man's Education*. New York: Knopf, 1967. See also Walpole.

Lindgren, E. J. "The Collection and Analysis of Folk-Lore." In *The Study of Society*, edited by F. C. Bartlett *et al.*, pp. 328-78. London: Kegan Paul, 1939.

Worth reading because it shows that there is a long history of collecting data through what are in effect interviews by students of folklore; I have not seen any effort to analyze their methods in general terms.

Lindzey. See Maccoby.

Lineberry. See Dexter.

Maccoby, Eleanor, and N. Maccoby. "The Interview: A Tool of Social Science." In *Handbook of Social Psychology*, edited by G. Lindzey. I, 449-87. Reading, Mass.: Addison Wesley, 1954.

MacPhee. See Jastak.

Madge, C. See Mass-Observation.

Madge, John. *The Tools of Social Science*. London: Longmans, Green, 1953; Garden City, N.Y.: Doubleday, Anchor Books, 1965.

> The chapter on interviewing, pp. 154-289, contains a masterly statement about different kinds of interviewing, major technical problems of interviewing, etc., and for this reason alone the text should, in my judgment, be used in any survey of research methods. (I would generally use it together with Webb and Webb; Webb, Campbell, Schwartz, and Sechrest; and Sjoberg and Nett.) The chapter on observation, pp. 120-53, does a good job of making clear that observation is a central skill; but it is ironic that Madge says more than four times as much about the methods of interviewing as about methods of observation!

Manning, Peter K. "Problems in Interpreting Interview Data." *Sociology and Social Research*, LI (1967), 302-16. Based in part upon Manning's Ph.D. thesis, "Occupational Types and Organized Medicine: Physician's Attitudes towards the American Medical Association," Duke University, 1966.

March. See Scott.

Marshall, S. L. A. *Pork-Chop Hill: The American Fighting Men in Korea.* New York: Morrow, 1956, pp. 16-17.

Describes a technique of reconstructing small-scale military movements shortly after the event by getting information from all able-bodied survivors in front of one another; Marshall alleges that rank made no difference!

Mason. See Gross.

Mass-Observation. *First Year's Work, 1937-38.* Edited by Charles Madge and Tom Harrisson. London: Lindsay Drummond, 1938.

This reports a singularly impressive plan and some unfortunately neglected accomplishments in relating interviewing, participant observation, and what Webb *et al.* call unobtrusive measures.

I expect that the present volume may be used as a text in courses on data collection and research. Were I to use it in this fashion myself, an excellent test question would be to ask for comment on the following from p. 66 of Madge and Harrisson: "Mass-Observation has always assumed that its untrained observers would be subjective cameras each with his or her own individual distortion. They tell us not what society is like, but what it looks like to them. An Observer's social point of view is decided in the first place by himself, in the second place by other people. In so far as it is decided by himself, it will tend to be exceptional . . . but in so far as his point of view is decided by everyday relations with other people, it will tend to be normal, since these relations are normal."

_____. *The Pub and the People.* Chiefly by John Sommerfield. London: Victor Gollancz, 1943.

Mead, Margaret. "The New Isolationism," *American Scholar,* XXIV (1955), 378-82.

Merton, R., M. Fiske, and P. Kendall. *The Focused Interview*. Glencoe, Ill.: Free Press, 1956.

Milford, Nancy. "The Golden Dreams of Zelda Fitzgerald." *Harper's Magazine*, January, 1969, pp. 46-53.

An extremely interesting account of the difficulties of interviewing associates of those who have become in any way legendary; especially valuable for oral historians.

Mink. See Dixon.

Mintz, Sidney. *Worker in the Cane: A Puerto Rican Life History*. New Haven: Yale University Press, 1964.

Moore. See Bingham.

Morrissey, Charles. "Oral History Interviewing on the Kennedy Project." Reprinted here as Chapter IV.

Myrdal, Gunnar. *An American Dilemma*. Vol. II. New York: Harper, 1944. See Appendix 2, "A Methodological Note on Facts and Valuations in Social Science."

Nadel, S. F. "The Interview Technique in Social Anthropology." In *The Study of Society*, edited by F. C. Bartlett *et al.*, pp. 317-27. London: Kegan Paul, 1939.

A genuinely outstanding discussion, worth reading by all social scientists.

Nett. See Sjoberg.

Paul, Benjamin D. "Interview Techniques and Field Relationships." In *Anthropology Today*, edited by A. L. Kroeber, pp. 430-51. Chicago: University of Chicago Press, 1953.

Payne, Stanley. *The Art of Asking Questions*. Princeton, N.J.: Princeton University Press, 1951.

Peabody. See Dexter.

Phillips, Bernard S. *Social Research, Strategy and Tactics.* New York: Macmillan, 1966. Especially see Chapters I ("Introduction"), III ("Process of Inquiry"), IV ("Principles of Data Collection"), and VI ("Interviews").

Polsby, Nelson. *Community Power and Political Theory.* New Haven: Yale University Press, 1963. See also Hunter.

Pool, Ithiel de Sola. "The Symbols of Electoral Programs in France." Master's thesis, University of Chicago, 1939.

Pool, Ithiel de Sola, and Irwin Shulman. "Newsman's Fantasies, Audiences, and Newswriting." In *People, Society, and Mass Communications*, edited by L. A. Dexter and D. White, pp. 141-59. Reprinted with editorial comment from *Public Opinion Quarterly*, Vol. XXIII (1959). See also Bauer.

Pottle. See Boswell.

Powdermaker, Hortense. *Stranger and Friend: The Way of the Anthropologist.* New York: Norton, 1966.

This is a uniquely valuable book for anyone planning to use informants or, indeed, to interview; the Preface and Epilogue should probably be read first, and then the reports of her four field studies: in Lesu (stone-age), Mississippi (which should be compared with Dollard), Hollywood (the reasons why this was a relative failure should be worth reflection), and Copperbelt Africa. No other scholar to my knowledge has shown how, in several different studies, her relationships with informants and interviewees affected the way the study was conducted; thereby, Powdermaker makes it possible to evaluate and, allowing for changing situations, to replicate her procedures and her inquiries.

Prothro. See Dexter.

Quarantelli. See Bucher.

Reik, Theodor. *Listening with the Third Ear: The Inner Experience of a Psychoanalyst.* New York: Farrar Straus, 1949.

See also Lane's comment on this approach, cited above.

Richardson, Stephen A., Barbara S. Dohrenwend, and David Klein. *Interviewing: Its Form and Functions.* New York: Basic Books, 1965.

The most comprehensive review of interviewing procedure and literature.

Riesman, David. *Abundance for What? and Other Essays.* Garden City, N.Y.: Doubleday, 1964.

Republishes his valuable essays on "The Sociology of the Interview," "Orbits of Tolerance, Interviewers, and Elites," and "Interviewers, Elites, and Academic Freedom," on pp. 517-83. The last-mentioned covers his report on the Lazarsfeld-Thielens study of faculty attitudes toward academic freedom.

————. Introduction to *The Passing of Traditional Society: Modernizing the Middle East,* by D. Lerner. New York: Free Press, 1958.

This is perhaps the most illuminating of all Riesman's discussions of the interview for the specialized interviewer, for in it Riesman confronts most directly the problem of interviewer-interviewee relationship (in terms that need no explanation of the project itself).

————. "Some Observations on Interviewing in a State Mental Hospital." *Bulletin of the Menninger Clinic,* XXIII (1959), 7-19.

This is one of the few outstanding discussions of specialized interviewing.

————, ed. *American Journal of Sociology,* Vol. LXII (September, 1956). Special number on interviewing.

Riesman, David, and Mark Benney. "Asking and Answering." *Journal of Business,* XXIX (1956), 225-36.

Riesman, David, in collaboration with Reuel Denney and Nathan Glazer. *The Lonely Crowd: A Study of the Changing American Character.* New Haven: Yale University Press, 1950.

Riesman, David, and Nathan Glazer. *Faces in the Crowd.* New Haven: Yale University Press, 1952.

Robinson, James A. "Simulation and Games." In *The New Media and Education; Their Impact on Society,* edited by Peter H. Rossi and Bruce J. Biddle, pp. 93-135. Chicago: Aldine, 1966; Garden City, N.Y.: Doubleday, Anchor Books, 1967.

The discussion of how games may help in teaching led me to wonder whether interviewers could develop games as substitutes or auxiliaries in elite and specialized interviewing; I am told that no one has reported on this possibility.

————. "Survey Interviewing among Members of Congress." *Public Opinion Quarterly,* XXIV (1960), 127-38.

Roethlisberger, Fritz, and Wm. Dickson. *Management and the Worker.* Cambridge: Harvard University Press, 1939.

Rosenthal, Robert. *Experimenter Effects in Behavioral Research.* New York: Appleton-Century-Crofts, 1966.

Rosenthal, Robert, and Lenore Jacobson. *Pygmalion in the Classroom.* New York: Holt, Reinhart and Winston, 1966. Especially see pp. 164-82.

The best statement of the way in which expectancies, self-fulfilling prophecies, affect outcomes; to some degree, with all due modifications, expectancies may affect the interview and certainly do affect the interview *report.*

Rosow, Irving. "Interviewing British Psychiatrists." *Public Opinion Quarterly,* XXI (1957), 279-87.

Rossi. See Robinson.

Roy, Donald F. "The Role of the Researcher in the Study of Social Conflict: A Theory of Protective Response." *Human Organization,* XXIV (1956), 262-71.

Ryskamp. See Boswell.

St. Angelo. See Gray.

Salancik. See Webb, E.

Salter, James T. *Boss Rule, Portraits in City Politics.* New York: McGraw-Hill, 1935.

Schiller, Ferdinand C. S. *Logic for Use.* London: G. Bell & Sons, 1929. See Chapter V, "Relevance."

Shows the subjectivity, selectivity, and riskiness of relevance, and the essential part it plays in a modern approach to problematic situations, such as the interview.

Schippers, Donald J., and Adelaide G. Tusler. *A Bibliography of Oral History.* Mimeographed, 1967. Available from Knox Mellon, Treasurer, Oral History Association (Department of History, Immaculate Heart College, 2021 N. Western Avenue, Los Angeles, California, 90027), $1.00.

————. "The Literature of Oral History." In *The Second National Colloquium of Oral History,* edited by Louis Starr, pp. 33-40.

Schwartz, Morris S. "The Mental Hospital: The Research Person in the Disturbed Ward." In *Reflections on Community Studies*, edited by A. Vidich, J. Bensman, and M. Stein, pp. 85-118.

"The patients would not permit me to relate to them as objects . . . and this was also true of the staff. They would not let me . . . hide behind the role of neutral, distant observer. I had to expose myself as a human being before I was accepted as a sociologist" (p. 101). The significance of this situation and attitude for research observation and interviewing is discussed.

Schwartz, R. See Webb, E.

Scott, W. R. "Field Methods in the Study of Organizations." In *Handbook of Organizations*, edited by James G. March, pp. 261-304. Chicago: Rand McNally, 1966.

Contains one of the few theoretical discussions of how informants should be used and dealt with.

Sechrest. See Webb, E.

Shaw, Clifford R. *Jack-Roller: A Delinquent Boy's Own Story.* Chicago: University of Chicago Press, 1930.

Shulman. See Pool.

Silverman. See Garceau.

Sjoberg, Gideon, ed. *Ethics, Politics, and Social Research.* Cambridge, Mass.: Schenckman Publishing Co., 1967. See also Colvard, Daniels, Goldner.

————. "The Interviewee As Marginal Man." *Southwestern Social Science Quarterly*, XXXVIII (1957-58), 124-32.

Argues that marginal man may, as such, acquire perspective

not held by others. Defines and lists various types of marginal man.

Sjoberg, Gideon, and Roger Nett. *A Methodology for Social Research*. New York: Harper, 1968.

This text (together with the book by Sidney and Beatrice Webb) could be used profitably in any course in elite interviewing; the chapter on explanation is particularly useful, since interviewing is usually undertaken in order to help "explain" something (pp. 288-313). The chapter on "the dissemination of research findings" presents in very broad terms a judicious view on the ethical problems of research (pp. 214-45). The chapter dealing with interviewing (pp. 187-222) is also valuable, although I myself, after considerable reflection, believe that the "objectifying interview" which the authors recommend can only be realized under optimum circumstances (for reasons indicated in my discussion of covert interviewing, and by Dalton and by Roy).

Sommerfield. See Mass-Observation.

Starr, Louis. In *Oral History at Arrowhead*, edited by E. Dixon and J. V. Mink, pp. 19-26.

_____, ed. *The Second National Colloquium on Oral History*. Mimeographed, 1968. Available from Knox Mellon, Treasurer, Oral History Association (Department of History, Immaculate Heart College, 2021 N. Western Avenue, Los Angeles, California 90027), $3.00.

Includes a discussion of oral history by a group of historians (pp. 1-20), and reports on the John Foster Dulles project (pp. 73-81) and the George C. Marshall project (pp. 82-94).

Stebbing, L. Susan. *Thinking to Some Purpose*. Harmondsworth, Middlesex: Penguin Books, 1939.

Steffens, Lincoln. *The Autobiography of Lincoln Steffens*. 2 vols. New York: Harcourt, Brace, 1931.

Stein, Maurice R. "The Eclipse of Community: Some Glances at the Education of A Sociologist." In *Reflections on Community Studies*, edited by A. Vidich, J. Bensman, and M. Stein, pp. 207-32.

This is a discussion of the place of "personal responses in social inquiry" (p. 207) and in consequence a criticism of undue reliance upon the survey-oriented "objective" methodology of such sociologists as Lazarsfeld and Merton. The points are, if valid at all, still more significant for elite studies of the sort typically made by political scientists than for community studies in general.

Strauss. See Glaser.

Sutherland, Edwin H., ed. *The Professional Thief*. Chicago: University of Chicago Press, 1937.

Anyone interested in the historical development of the lengthy series of interviews would do well to study this; it would be desirable to have it replicated with more modern methods.

Thielens. See Lazarsfeld.

Thomas, W. I. *The Unadjusted Girl with Cases and Standpoint for Behavior Analysis*. Boston: Little, Brown, 1931.

Contains one of the numerous statements by Thomas of the "definition of the situation" approach to social reality, which underlies the current emphasis on interviewing.

Tusler. See Schippers.

Vidich, Arthur, J. Bensman, and M. R. Stein. *Reflections on Community Studies*. New York: Wiley, 1964.

Includes "The Springdale Case: Academic Bureaucrats and Sensitive Townspeople," by A. Vidich and J. Bensman, pp. 313-49. See also Whyte; Schwartz; Stein; Becker.

Vidich, Arthur, and J. Bensman. "Validity of Field Data." *Human Organization,* XIII (1954), 20-27.

Wahlke, John C., Heinz Eulau, Wm. Buchanan, and Leroy C. Ferguson. *The Legislative System: Explorations in Legislative Behavior.* New York: Wiley, 1962. See "Interview Procedures and Experiences," by Eulau and Wahlke, pp. 441-52. See also Hunt.

Walpole, Horace (4th Earl of Orford). *Correspondence with Sir Horace Mann,* 1742-1780. Yale Walpole Series, edited by W. S. Lewis *et al.,* Vols. 18-24. New Haven: Yale University Press, 1954-67.

Exemplifies in quintessential form the pleasure some knowledgeable people get out of being informants; also, Walpole's life lends depth to the conception of "marginal man" put forth in Sjoberg's article.

Ward, Robert E., ed. *Studying Politics Abroad; Field Research in the Developing Areas.* Boston: Little, Brown, 1964. See also Weiner.

Watson, David Lindsay. *The Study of Human Nature.* Yellow Springs, Ohio: Antioch Press, 1953. Especially see pp. 149-71 (on reading physiognomy, etc.) and pp. 172-211 (on literature and social investigation).

Wax, Rosalie H. "Reciprocity as a Field Technique." *Human Organization,* XI (1958), 34-37.

Webb, Eugene, and Jerry Salancik. "The Interview or The Only Wheel in Town." *Journalism Monograph* no. 2 (November, 1966). Association for Education in Journalism, School of Communications, University of Texas.

Indispensable; greatly enriches both Chapter VI and Chapter II in this book.

Webb, Eugene, D. Campbell, R. Schwartz, and L. Sechrest. *Unobtrusive Measures: Nonreactive Research in the Social Sciences.* Chicago: Rand McNally, 1966.

Indispensable in considering alternatives to the interview.

Webb, Sidney, and Beatrice Webb (Baron and Lady Passfield). *Methods of Social Study.* 1932. Reissued. New York: A. M. Kelley, 1968.

As the authors point out, their work has been largely concerned with the comparative study of specific institutions in one country. Perhaps because my own work (and that of, for example, most political scientists specializing in Congress or state government) has the same concern with the study of specific institutions in one country, I find (and I think my colleagues in these areas will find) this is still extremely valuable as a text. It would be on my reading list for any course in elite or specialized interviewing.

Weiner, Myron. "Political Interviewing." In *Studying Politics Abroad,* edited by Robert E. Ward.

A very useful article for anyone engaged in studying political, or for that matter organizational, problems anywhere by use of the interview.

Wheeler, Elmo. *Sizzlemanship: New Tested Selling Sentences.* Englewood Cliffs, N.J.: Prentice-Hall, 1940.

A presentation of how to get favorable answers from potential purchasers by the adroit phrasing of questions; might be useful in (a) getting interviews, and (b) identifying questions which in fact are leading but are not recognized as such.

White. See Dexter.

Whiteman. See Jastak.

Whyte, William Foote. "On Asking Indirect Questions." *Human Organization*, XV (1956), 21-23. See also Dean.

_____. "The Slum: On the Evolution of Street Corner Society." In *Reflections on Community Studies*, edited by A. Vidich, J. Bensman, and M. Stein, pp. 3-70. (Approximately the same as the Appendix to the new revised edition of *Street Corner Society*.)

An outstanding demonstration of how informants are selected, nearly unique in its depiction of the relationship between clarification of a problem and the utilization of informants.

_____. *Street Corner Society*. Rev. ed. Chicago: University of Chicago Press, 1955.

Williams, Josephine J. "Patients and Prejudice: Lay Attitudes towards Women Physicians." *American Journal of Sociology*, LI (1946), 283-87.

Williams, Thomas Rhys. *Field Methods in the Study of Culture*. New York: Holt, Rinehart and Winston, 1967.

See also Beattie; Powdermaker; Whyte ("The Slum"); Paul; and Nadel for other discussions of such field methods.

INDEX